**WHISPERING
OAKS**

"Travel is fatal to prejudice, bigotry and narrow-mindedness, and many of our people need it sorely... Broad, wholesome, charitable views... can not be acquired by vegetating in one's little corner of the earth."

Mark Twain, The Innocents Abroad, 1869

Traveling Solo

on a shoestring

Quay Marie Estocin

Traveling Solo on a Shoestring
By Q. Marie Estocin

Print ISBN: 978-0-9893000-0-1
eBook ISBN: 978-0-9893000-2-5

Interior Design by Fusion Creative Works, www.fusioncw.com
Cover Design and Art by Kathy Estocin-Foley

Whispering Oaks Press, LLC
Whisperingoakspress@gmail.com
708 Gravenstein Hwy N #242
Sebastopol, CA 95472

WHISPERING
OAKS

First Printing
Printed in the United States of America

For my granddaughters, Storm and Rowan,
encouraging you to travel.

Quay Marie Estocin

Introduction

In the pages of this book I want to share with you the fulfillment of a dream I had for years; a dream to travel, to see the world.

It doesn't matter if you are twenty, forty, or in your late fifties as I was. What does matter is the desire and the willingness to let go of all the preconceived ideas that kept you from traveling.

What kept me from this dream for so many years? Fear. That's right, fear. The fear of traveling alone, of not being able to afford it, of leaving my family for an extended period of time, and so on.

While browsing in a book store, six months or a year before my trip, one title jumped out at me. *"Feel the Fear and Do It Anyway."* I purchased the book and the title became my motto for living life.

I want to tell you how my trip around the world came about; give you a few tips for traveling; and share some of my experiences with you. Perhaps you think taking a journey for a long period of time is out of the question. Wrong! I am here to tell you that if you have a desire to travel, whether it's to see the world, to see the United States, or to just explore the state in which you live, it is possible.

I have traveled to many places. I have seen much of the United States, some of Canada, parts of Europe, Australia, New Zealand, Central and South America. Some of these excursions were with a traveling companion.

But what happens when you don't have a traveling companion? You just go!

Considering Traveling

In the summer of 1992, while visiting my family in California, I had lunch with a close lady friend. During our conversation the topic turned to travel. We had both wanted to take a big trip. We talked about going to Europe the next fall.

In the spring of 1993 I called my friend to see how life was treating her. I found out that she was unable to join me on this trip. I hung up the phone feeling greatly disappointed. Would I have to forget my plans to travel? Maybe I could find someone else to join me, or... could I go alone? This last thought caught my attention. Go alone. Well, why not? That would be an adventure.

As I contemplated that idea, another thought slowly took shape. Why not travel as I had wanted to for years, and take an around-the-world trip?

After digesting and contemplating ideas for a few days, I found myself at the desk of a local travel agent, seeking information about an around-the-world airline ticket. She said that it was possible to get one, but there were a few restrictions on such a ticket. I would have to complete my travels within one year; I could change the dates along the way, but not the departure date, without a fee; and I must always be traveling in the same direction. In other words, if I chose to travel east to west, I could go north or south but always in a westerly direction.

In order to quote a price she needed to know in which direction I wanted to travel and into which cities I wanted to fly. Not having any idea how to answer these questions, I asked her for a world map to take home with me. At home, I hung the large map on my kitchen wall. I pulled up a chair, put my reading glasses on, and sat down to study this big world of ours.

As I scanned the map, Vietnam caught my attention; Vietnam, where I lost my husband in 1967. He had been shot down while flying a combat mission during the Vietnam conflict. He was listed as Missing in Action. And in November of 1977 the government changed his status to Killed in Action. He is still on the unaccounted-for list in Washington, D.C. all these years later.

The thought of going to Vietnam had entered my mind many times, but was I ready? As I looked at the map, I thought, "I'm now ready to face that painful part of my past. Just like that, my decision was made. I would take this trip, and I would go alone. Japan seemed like a good place to start as I worked my way toward Vietnam.

After a couple of weeks of adding and subtracting countries, I came up with a tentative itinerary and headed back to the travel agency.

Travel Agent

Finding the best travel agent, for you, may take some shopping around. It did for me. My first agent put her travels before doing research for me, so I went to another.

The second company took my list and came up with a quote that was not in my budget. Then a friend told me of another company that she felt was very competent and shopped for the best price for their clients.

I chose the third travel agent because the quote was in my budget. She and her consultant supplied me with information that not only saved me hundreds of dollars, but added adventure to my trip by suggesting different areas to visit in southeast Asia that I would not have thought of exploring. This travel agent gave me a few brochures on some of my destinations and suggested I pick up a travel book. A good travel book is essential. I will cover that later.

Leaving the ticket arrangements in the capable hands of my agent, I now directed my energy toward the many other tasks that had to be done before the departure date.

Today, many of us use our frequent flyer miles, talk to different airlines, and Google for cheap airfares for our flights, instead of using a travel agent. But if you are thinking about taking a trip around the world, you must use a travel agent. Some of the restrictions may have changed and a travel agent will know that information or if they don't know they will know where to find it.

Helpful Hints

When the travel bug hits, you never know where you might land. Having a valid passport on hand is always a good idea. If you do not have a current one, check with your local post office for the application procedure in your area.

When traveling out of the country, Foreign Entry Requirements are important to know. You can most likely Google them and find out what you need to know for the countries you are interested in visiting.

If you want to travel on a budget, the book I found to be the most comprehensive was *Lonely Planet*. *Lonely Planet* guide books cover every accessible part of Asia, Australia, the Pacific, South America, Africa, the Middle East, Europe, and parts of North America. Now there are many other books that may be better; which one you pick us is your choice.

Travel books take up space and weight. Bring your favorite book with your on your journey and purchase others along the way. *Lonely Planet* guide books are distributed worldwide. With all the technology we have today you could take a tablet or Kindle and have a variety of books at your disposal without extra weight. You can get these through amazon.com or any bookstore.

Next, an International Youth Hostel card will help keep the cost of lodging to a minimum. You do not have to be young to enjoy these inexpensive accommodations; they might offer a reduced membership price for seniors. It is a comfortable and safe way to meet fellow travelers from all over the world. You can Google IYH for information and membership.

A friend of mine recommended that I join United States Servas, an international travelers' organization with members in most parts of the world. The motto of this unique club is: "Build Peace Through Understanding". Servas invites individuals of all ethnic backgrounds to be traveler, host, or both. Look at their website: www.usservas.org

I joined Servas before leaving the U.S. and had wonderful gratifying experiences with hosts in Japan, India, and Switzerland. A number of the friends I made through Servas I am still in contact with today. The time and experiences we shared are worth their weight in gold and will remain in my heart forever.

You are probably wondering about your monthly bills. This is a very important factor, especially if you are going on an extended trip. When traveling for a long period of time it is important to leave your financial matters with someone you trust. And you can have all your monthly payments taken out of your checking account automatically. Check with your vendors for these procedures.

A power-of-attorney is a good idea. If something happens to you, someone will need to act on your behalf. And, by all means, update your will. Some of you may choose more than one person to handle these delicate affairs for you.

If you own your home or condo you may not want to leave it vacant even for a short period of time. Many reliable house-sitters can be found by word of mouth and through friends or families. You can hire a reputable management company to rent out or just oversee your residence for a long or even a short period of time. By just packing up your personal things and locking them in an extra room, closet, or safe-deposit box, you will insure their safety. I had my mail sent to my daughter's home, which was convenient as she was taking care of my bills. I found a person who paid me a nominal fee to live in and oversee my home. This arrangement helped both of us financially. He moved in a couple of months before I left and when I departed, I was confident that he would take good care of my home.

Last, but not least, if you are traveling on a limited budget, and carry a pack on your back, you need to be fairly fit. Either begin walking, biking, or running on your own, or consider joining a gym for a month or so before your trip begins. Being fit can make all the difference between whether your trip is enjoyable or not. Feeling physical discomfort can distract from the joys of traveling. A good pair of walking shoes is another must-have.

After completing these tasks and knowing all your affairs are in order, you can rest assured that when you return, all will be well and that your are ready to go traveling!

Beginning in the United States

In mid-August I left my home in Sandpoint, Idaho by car en route to Los Angeles where my trip around the world would originate. I traveled the coastal route out of Portland, staying in hostels and with friends along the way. It was a beautiful drive and a perfect prelude to my adventure in traveling alone.

In Los Angeles I visited my three daughters and stayed with my oldest daughter and son-in-law and spent time getting re-acquainted with my young granddaughter. Clara, then six months old, was just beginning to sit up and was trying to crawl. My emotions were mixed. I recognized feelings of sadness to be missing much of her growth, but also feelings of excitement to be given this opportunity to see the world.

As I contemplated what to take along, my daughter, Kathy, gave me a lovely book in which to keep a journal of my travels. On the front cover of the journal book I pasted an affirmation from my daily calendar:

*"While I enjoy my trip around the world I am Divinely pro-
tected and guided. Everyone is helpful. I stay within my budget
and have a wonderful time."*

Keeping a journal turned out to be a very important part of
my journey.

As I packed my backpack I took mostly lightweight clothing.
I chose tops and shorts or slacks that could be washed and be
discarded down the way. I did not take any medication at that
time so that was not a problem. I did pack some of my favorite
vitamins that could be replaced along the way.

I checked my itinerary. I was pleased and excited about this
adventure I would be going on: Los Angeles to Tokyo; Tokyo to
Taipei, Taipei to Hong Kong; Hong Kong to Bangkok, Thailand.
In Bangkok I would purchase my ticket to Hanoi, Vietnam.
My travel agent advised me that this would save money. Then
Bangkok to Singapore; Singapore to the Island of Bali, Denpensar
to Indonesia; then from Jakarta (on the Island of Java) in Indonesia
to Bombay, India. My next flight would be from New Delhi,
India to Cairo, Egypt; Cairo to Zurich, Switzerland; Zurich to
London; London to Miami; Miami to Los Angeles. The changes
made along the way will be discussed later.

The around-the-world airline ticket allowed me to change the
dates anytime I wanted. For instance, if I chose to stay for a longer
or shorter period of time than what was indicated on the ticket,
all I had to do was call the airlines and change it, depending on
availability. I would be flying on Singapore Airlines, Swiss Air. and
then back to the United State on Delta.

At the Japanese Travel Service in Los Angeles I purchased a Japanese Railway Pass (JR Pass). This pass could not be purchased once I arrived in Japan. It was invaluable as trains in Japan were quite expensive. You might check into this as it may have changed. That office also gave me a list of budget hotels in the Tokyo area. I would be arriving at Narita, Tokyo's International Airport, in the early evening. Narita is about an an hour and a half from the city center. I decided to book a reservation near the airport for my first night in Japan. I sent a fax to the Skycourt Hotel in Narita which supplies a free shuttle bus to and from the airport. My confirmation arrived the next day. These days you can just email them.

I wrote a Servas member in Tokyo before leaving the USA and received a reply before I left. Back in the 90s no one had email, and now so many of the questions and answers can be handled by email.

The Servas host wrote that I was welcome to stay, but she had a very small apartment and hoped I would not mind. I did not mind. The reason for joining Servas was not only to save money, but also to taste the flavor of the countries from a local's point of view. Getting acquainted with my Servas hosts was very rewarding. Becoming friends and staying in touch with my hosts into the future was a big plus for being a Servas traveler.

Knowing my letter would not reach Japan before I arrived, I phoned and accepted her generous offer to stay in her apartment.

Departure

Okay, close your eyes and now let's pretend you are sitting in the waiting room of Singapore Airlines in Los Angeles, California. From the loudspeaker you hear, "All aboard, please, for Singapore Airline's flight No. 11, non-stop to Tokyo, Japan." Is your heart beating just a little faster? I'll tell you mine was. Take a few deep breaths as you board the plane.

Fasten your seat belt, because you are on your way to an adventure of a lifetime.

Japan

After a long but pleasant fourteen-hour flight, the big Singapore Airlines jet landed at Narita International Airport. The flight attendants had been very friendly and the food was good. I was given a pillow and a light blanket for my comfort. When I was leaving the plane, I asked one of the flight attendants if I could have the light blanket; she smiled and gave me an affirmative nod.

Once off the airplane, I retrieved my backpack and sailed through customs and the passport check.

Finding the platform for the shuttle bus was easy enough. I boarded and in about twenty minutes I found myself standing in my small, but very neat and clean room at the Skycourt Hotel. On a hanger was a blue kimono and on the floor a pair of Japanese slippers. I quickly undressed and headed for the shower. The bathroom was tiny with only enough space for a small shower and a commode. This was the last commode I would see for awhile. From here on I encountered mostly Japanese toilets, which women must squat to use.

After showering I threw on the kimono and took a photograph of myself. I was in awe. I was in Tokyo, Japan!

The next day, a bus ride into the city, usually an an hour and a half ride, took about two hours. The streets were jammed with morning rush hour traffic. I got off at the Shinjuku Station as instructed by my Servas host when I had spoken to her that morning.

She advised me to go on the Keio Line and take a subway. I found the Keio Line and walked up to the ticket counter. The man at the window did not speak English and all the signs were in Japanese. I found this to be normal in Japan. Very few people speak English and there are very few signs in English. I discovered (from a guide book) that if I wrote what I wanted to say and showed it to someone, I would be helped. Most Japanese read and write English. They are taught English in school at an academic level, but not at a conversational level. Today there may be more people who speak English.

While I stood there contemplating what to do, I noticed four young girls and asked if they spoke English. One of them answered she did a little, so I wrote where I wanted to go on a paper and handed it to her. To my amazement they were going to the same place. One of the girls showed me how to purchase a ticket from a machine and we were on our way. This was just the beginning of a trip that seemed to be Divinely guided.

At my destination the girls helped me to find a phone, showed me how to use it and which coins were required. I called my hostess. She said, "Wait right there...I'll be there shortly."

Ten minutes later a rather short, attractive Japanese girl arrived. "Welcome to Japan," she said. After a few moments of conversation she led me toward a long flight of stairs. As we ascended the stairs I realized how heavy my backpack was. I was huffing and puffing by the time we reached the top. I was pleased when she said her mother was waiting with a car.

Seeing Japan was interesting and intriguing. My late husband had spoken of his time in Japanese ports during his numerous cruises to the Far East. I was now experiencing first-hand this country that I had only seen in photographs or read about in magazines or books. The people of this small country comprise the strongest memories that are still with me. It wasn't just my Servas hosts who were so unforgettable, but the Japanese people who helped me on the streets or in the subways as well.

From Tokyo I took a train to Kyoto. Here I stayed with two different Servas hosts. The first one, a young high school English teacher, has since married and moved to the United States. She and her husband lived in Mississippi for a number of years, but I have now lost contact with them. After spending one night at her apartment I was invited to the home of another Servas host. This was a very friendly Japanese couple, close to my age. The husband spoke very good English, but the wife's English was limited.

The first evening the husband left for a business meeting, leaving his wife and me alone. Since we could not converse we just smiled a lot during the delicious Japanese dinner of fresh vegetables that she prepared in a soy sauce and served over rice.

After dinner she took me into their sitting room and displayed the photographs of her family. I did the same. Then I took out the

Christmas stocking I was knitting for my son-in-law and began
to knit. Seeing this, she brought out a very large box filled with
beautiful sweaters that she and one of her daughters had knitted.

Turning on the television, she took out a sweater she was working on and sat down on the floor near me. Both sets of needles
began to click. When her husband returned he found two women
sitting in silence, but obviously enjoying each other's presence.
In spite of the language barrier, she and I became friends. Her
husband said later that he hoped they could come to the United
States some day to visit me, and I could help his wife with her
English. I told them it would be an honor to have them visit and I
would be more than eager to help her speak the English language.

The beautiful, old city of Kyoto has so much charm. I could
feel the history as I roamed through its numerous temples. I felt
more relaxed with its slower pace; not as much hustle and bustle
as Tokyo with its crowded streets and subways.

A few days later I booked a seat on a train to Osaka. My
Servas host in Osaka was a lovely Japanese businesswoman and
her twelve-year-old daughter. Their apartment was small but neat
and comfortable. I slept on a mat on the living room floor as is
customary in Japan. I did not mind sleeping on the floor. Meeting
the people and experiencing the different lifestyles was all part of
my great adventure.

Each morning before leaving for her job, Takako, my hostess,
made breakfast. She prepared rice the night before in a crock pot,
so when we awoke it was steaming hot. With the rice we were
given the choice of adding milk or a package of already-packaged
seasoning. I chose the seasoning but her daughter chose milk. For

my sightseeing excursions she made little balls of rice with the powdered seasoning and soy sauce. She placed these in a styrofoam box with a small green salad and sometimes a hard-boiled egg or fish. I appreciated the lunches immensely.

My guide book, as well as my hostess, suggested the following excursions: The Osaka Castle, a puppet show, and going to a Sushi bar. The only place I explored was the Osaka Castle. That is a must! The extraordinary old castle is situated on a moat. The castle, even though rather small, is lovely. The grounds are beautiful and spacious. The day I was there it rained but it was very impressive even on this dull, dreary day. I only stayed with them for four nights and three days but I felt like I had known them for years.

It was time to move on, so I took a train to Nara. I stayed in a youth hostel instead of with a Servas member. The Nara youth hostel was one of the neatest and cleanest places I encountered during my travels and it only cost eighteen American dollars back in 1993. It would certainly be more costly today.

I spent only one day there visiting the Nara Park, home of the famous Kasuga Grand Shrine. At the entrance to the park area there are hundreds of deer running free. And you can buy food for them. Once I fed them they would not leave me alone! So my advice is to see the park and then feed the deer.

That evening at the hostel I met two young women from Germany. One was a doctor and the other was in her last year of veterinary college. Kirsten, the girl studying to be a veterinarian, and I discovered we were both taking the train back to Tokyo the next morning. We decided to travel together.

Kirsten was on her way to meet a German girlfriend who was living and working in Tokyo for a few months. I was traveling back there to catch a flight to Taiwan. We agreed to share a room in Tokyo. We searched for a hostel or guest house in our book, the only inexpensive lodgings in Japan. We figured we could share a room in a guest house.

While changing trains in Kyoto we called ahead for lodging. After a number of calls we found a guest house with a double room available. It was twenty American dollars back then. We told the English-speaking man we would take it. When we arrived in Tokyo we found the guest house to be run down. But it was about 9:30 in the evening, too late to search for something better.

We saw some men in the downstairs lounge of the small hotel who looked a little shady, so we went to our room and locked the door. We didn't come out until the next morning. When we spoke to the "shady characters" at breakfast we happily found they were just like us, visitors to Japan trying to stay within their budget. The white guy was interviewing for an acting job. His traveling companion was as American girl who had spoken to us as we entered our room the night before. Because she had black and blue marks on her arms and neck, seeing her added more fuel to our already vivid imaginations. During our conversations over breakfast we discovered she has a black belt in karate and was in Japan to participate in karate competitions. No wonder she was black and blue!

We left there laughing at our ignorance. We had allowed our imaginations to run wild. We thought the worst about these people before we knew anything about them. This was a valuable lesson for me to learn early in my trip around the world.

From the guest house, Kirsten and I took a subway to Shinjuku Train Station. Once there we stored our backpacks in a locker and went to find the friend she was meeting in Tokyo. The girls asked me to join them for the day. I gladly accepted. I was booked on an early morning flight to Taiwan and was staying, once again, at the Skycourt Hotel near the airport. It was not necessary to take the train to Narita until that evening.

Exploring Tokyo with friends was so much more fun, especially friends with such a keen sense of humor. Even though these girls were in their twenties and I was in my fifties, we all giggled like teenagers.

We went to a sushi bar in the shopping center for lunch. The restaurant had a conveyer belt laden with dishes of all varieties of sushi. We had a wonderful time choosing a dish and not knowing what it was. The cashier figured out how much we owed by the color of the dish and how many we had. It was not as expensive as we expected it to be. The total cost us about ten American dollars each. Can you believe the prices back then?

After lunch we took the subway to Yoyogi Park, the site of the International Music Festival. Each Sunday over 100,000 people visit this park. The musicians as well as the spectators were dressed outrageously. Many wore their hair long, or teased high on their heads in a variety of colors from bright purple to orange. Leather and spikes were popular as were ostrich feathers. The park made Venice Beach in Los Angeles look like Sunday school. The music was so loud it was deafening. No conversation here, just a lot of laughs.

Our heads still pounding from the loud music, we took another subway and got off near the Hard Rock Cafe. I promised my youngest daughter I would bring back as many Hard Rock Cafe t-shirts as possible. Finding t-shirts for Suzie became a challenge on my travels.

When it was time to catch the train to the hotel in Narita, the girls offered to accompany me and insisted on carrying my bags. I was so used to doing everything for myself that allowing them to carry the bags felt strange. But they insisted, so I gave in and allowed the rare bit of pampering.

It was a rather long walk, often up and down stairs, making my newly purchased wheels for my large backpack useless. Upon reaching the train I hugged my two friends warmly and thanked them for such a fun day and for carrying my bags.

I left Japan the next morning with many fond memories. I was leaving behind a number of new friends. We exchanged addresses so we could keep in touch and hoped the bonds we forged would not be forgotten.

Now, all these years later, I have lost contact with all the wonderful people I met and spent time with in Japan.

Taiwan

In Taiwan I noticed a difference in appearance between the Japanese and the Chinese people. The Japanese seemed small and petite whereas the Chinese were short but large-boned. I found the Chinese accents more difficult to understand. Although many more spoke English, it seemed nasal and a little choppy.

I was most pleased when I noticed that most of their signs were in English. I had no trouble finding a money exchanger and bus transportation into the city.

When the bus dropped me off in downtown Taipei, I stepped into a city filled with noise from cars, motor scooters, and people. There were more little scooters than cars. The motor scooters parked as well as drove on the sidewalks.

I had to be very alert so as not to be run down by one as I strolled along. The dust and pollution were almost unbearable. After clean Japan, this was a nightmare!

The city was too congested and polluted to walk the short distance to my hotel so I hailed a taxi. I gave him the address of the Prince Hotel and sat back and breathed a sigh of relief as he expertly maneuvered through the worst traffic jam I had ever experienced.

Taipei was so polluted that I could not walk around the streets to see the sights as I had in Japan. I noticed a sign in the hotel for day sightseeing excursions, so I eagerly signed up. Group tours are not my favorite way to see a city, but for the safety of my lungs I knew that was the best way to see Taipei.

On the city tour we were taken to the Palace Museum, which had a remarkable collection. A group tour does not give one a fraction of the time needed to really see and appreciate the many beautiful artifacts and treasures housed there. I spent most of my time roaming through the large display of snuff bottles, which resemble exquisite perfume bottles. I don't remember why they called them snuff bottles.

The North Coast Tour took us to Keeling City and its harbor. Nearby we explored the Natural Rock Park. My favorite rock formation was the «Queen's Head». This Park is on the shores of the Pacific Ocean. As I gazed out at the sea I remember thinking, "My daughters are on the other side of this huge body of water." As I sat there thinking of them, tears came to my eyes. Traveling solo did get lonely at times, but in a few moments the excitement of traveling returned.

That evening I went on an evening tour. Our first stop was for dinner at a Mongolian restaurant where you choose what you want from an array of fresh vegetables, fish, chicken, pork, or beef. Then you add a variety of sauces for seasoning. This is then given to a chef to cook on a large grill. You can eat as much as you want. The food was delicious and healthy.

We then visited the Grand Hotel This magnificent structure was built by Madam Chaing Kai Shek. Once it was the tallest building in Taiwan although now it is overshadowed by skyscrapers. However, it is one of the last remaining examples of Chinese classical architecture. The ceiling of the hotel lobby is exquisite.

Our last stop was the Night Market. Visiting this large marketplace is a must while in Taipei. There are many vendors with just about anything one might want to purchase. While there, don't pass up "Snake Alley". We watched a man take a snake from a large barrel and clip its mouth closed until it suffocated. When the snake was apparently dead, he made an incision and took out some of the reptile's insides. From this he squeezed enough blood to fill a glass already half full with rice wine. The people of Taiwan believe this potion to be very powerful medicine which cures many illnesses. They also believe it to be an aphrodisiac. A lady, tall for a Chinese woman, waited patiently, with her money in hand, during the entire procedure. Then she took the glass the man offered her, quickly drank the "magic potion," and paid him before scurrying off.

For me this was a ghastly experience, from the treatment of the snake to the consumption of the potion, but it is a belief and a custom of the people of Taiwan. Who am I to judge it?

My visit to Taipei does not entice me to return. However, I suspect there are many more interesting places in and around the city that I did not see in the short time I was there.

Hong Kong

As the airplane approached Kowloon Island, I noticed the airport was surrounded by water and in the distance, towering skyscrapers jutted into view. Upon landing, I collected my bags and trudged over to the new YMCA on Kowloon Island where I had a reservation. Upon check-in the clerk explained that the Y is available to people who have just arrived in Hong Kong and the stay is limited to one week.

I rode the elevator to my room on the fifth floor. The small dormitory room was furnished with four bunk beds. There was a separate locker and lock for each of the bunks. The Y was a brand-new building at that time so it was very clean. I left my backpack in the locker and went out to explore the area.

The Y is just across the street from the harbor and the Star Ferry, which connects Kowloon to Hong Kong Island. The eight-minute ride cost about 20 cents U.S. in 1993.

As I walked to the wall at the harbor I was struck by the beautiful skyline of Hong Kong. I sat on the retaining wall and allowed it all to sink in.

After dinner I returned to the harbor to see Hong Kong Central at night. Colorful lights reach the tops of the highest buildings and twinkle their reflections in the water, making Hong Kong Central seem even closer than it already was. This sight is so sensational it is impossible for me to describe adequately.

During the next week I busied myself seeing more of Kowloon, crossing on the ferry over to Hong Kong Island and exploring Hong Kong Central.

The travel agent whom I used for the trip advised obtaining most of the visas I would need for the entire trip in Hong Kong because they are less expensive there. This did not work out as she thought it would. I suggest that if you have time, get your visas before leaving the United States, even though they might be more expensive. Because while you are obtaining a visa, the consulates keeps your passport, making it impossible to leave Hong Kong. I wasted some very precious time waiting to get my passport back and could not venture into China for a few days as I had planned. Hong Kong was not part of China at that time.

I knew, before arriving in Hong Kong, that I would not be able to stay with a Servas member. Hong Kong offers only Day Hosts, who help with information or meet you for lunch or dinner. The island has limited square footage so most people live in small apartments with no extra room for guests.

I contacted only one host in the three weeks I was in Hong Kong. We met for dinner. She was a cute Chinese girl who spoke English very well. She had been to the United States a year or so before, so we had a lot to discuss. She chose a typical Chinese restaurant and ordered for both of us. It was a delightful evening.

During my three-week stay in Hong Kong, I had seen much of the beautiful city and explored many of the surrounding islands. I had procured all the visas I needed, except for Egypt; I would purchase that in India.

The next segment was one of the prime motivations for my entire trip and I knew it would be emotional.

Vietnam

California's San Joaquin Valley glistens in the April sun. It is an idyllic time to be in the midst of the expansive blue skies, before soaring temperatures distract from the natural beauty. The spring of 1967 brought with it an intruder to the quiet lives of Navy families in the area. That intruder chose to arrive in a long black sedan, much like death itself, that looked out of place in the otherwise bright surroundings.

That intruder pulled into my driveway one morning in late April, bringing terrible news. The Captain of Lemoore Naval Air Station emerged from the ominous black sedan, summoned me to the door and told me that my husband had been shot down in North Vietnam. He was missing in action. I panicked. My world would never be the same. My happy life was over. What would I say to our three daughters?

Then I remembered that the Captain said "missing in action", not killed. A glimmer of hope began to spark in my heart. Maybe my husband would be back home with me and our daughters in the not-too-distant future.

Ten-and-a-half years later, the United States Navy declared my husband, Captain Michael J. Estocin, killed in action and gave November 10, 1977 as a presumptive date of death. He was placed on the "unaccounted for" list, where his name remains today.

The glimmer of hope I felt back in 1967 slowly vanished. Hope was replaced with feelings of fear, anger, and resentment toward both my husband and the Vietnamese people; toward my husband for volunteering to fly the hop that day, that fateful day being the last day on the line, ending a seven-month separation. I misguidedly held the Vietnamese people responsible for my misfortune.

In 1993 it was almost twenty-seven years since that tragic day. I was on my way to Vietnam to heal my wounds; to say a final good bye to my husband; to visit the country; to meet the people. Then, I felt that I could see the rest of the world with a lighter heart.

From Hong Kong I boarded a plane to Bangkok, Thailand. My stay in Bangkok was only long enough to pick up a visa for Vietnam. The requests for the visa, a guide and/or interpreter, and hotel reservations were made through the U.S. government and the Vietnamese Ambassador before leaving the United States.

In the fall of 1993, it was not easy for an American to obtain a visa for entering Vietnam. But because of the assistance that I received from the U.S. government and Vietnamese government, the visa was waiting when I arrived in person at the Vietnamese Embassy in Bangkok.

Before my departure from Los Angeles I was informed that all arrangements had been taken care of and someone would be there to meet me when I arrived in Hanoi.

For the journey to Vietnam, the ambassador advised me to bring American currency. Vietnam would not accept American credit cards. At that time the economic boycott was still in effect. Only American dollars would be accepted. I was pleased to learn later during my travels that the boycott was lifted.

Sitting in the Bangkok airport waiting for my flight, I felt the anxiety build. I wished my three daughters were with me. They had always been with me in the past on important occasions concerning their father. But not this time. This I must do alone.

Finally I heard the announcement to board the aircraft. I took my assigned seat and fastened my seat belt. A few minutes later the plane taxied down the runway and began to gain altitude. It was difficult to believe that I was actually on an airplane bound for Hanoi, Vietnam. Just the name flooded my mind with painful memories. For years I had been harboring such negative feelings toward this country and its people. Now I was actually going there, not to find the remains of my husband, but to let go and to find inner peace. As we made our approach into Hanoi's International Airport I felt nervous. Had someone received the message of my flight number and time of arrival?

I breezed through immigration, claimed my luggage, and got in line for customs. My mind was racing with thoughts of being stranded in Hanoi. Just as I felt the thoughts reaching the level of panic, I looked out the window. In the crowded "waiting for arrivals" area, there was a young Vietnamese man holding a sign with

"Mrs. Estocin" written on it. I was so relieved. I waved frantically so he would know I saw him.

Now finished with customs, I hoisted my backpack onto my back and quickly joined the young man. He introduced himself in almost flawless English as Vu Viet Dung. The last name, which he goes by, is pronounced "Zoom" in English. Zoom is with the Ministry of Foreign Affairs in Hanoi and was to be my guide and interpreter for the next five days.

Also meeting my plane was an American from the U. S. State Department. He was associated with the U. S. Joint Task Force, which has its compound in Hanoi. He invited me to come to the compound to meet Lt. Colonel John Cray, the commander of the Joint Task Force, and his crew while I was in Hanoi. This Task Force was formed a few years prior to help search for the men still missing and unaccounted for in Vietnam.

A few minutes later the American left and Zoom escorted me to the waiting car and driver. As we drove along, Zoom began to fill me in on the tentative itinerary for the week. I listened with one ear while looking out the car window at the roads, which were very narrow and in great need of repair. As a passenger, I found the ride both scary and exciting. The driver was honking the car horn while dodging cows, pedestrians, people riding bicycles and motor bikes, and water buffalo pulling carts.

The driver and Zoom seemed totally unconcerned with all this activity. Zoom kept on talking and the driver miraculously maneuvered the car through all that commotion.

Fascinated, I observed the people. They were wearing "coolie" hats as they maneuvered the carts along the streets, pulled by giant water buffalo. This was what I had expected from television coverage of Vietnam I had seen over twenty years ago; but I had anticipated this scene to be in the remote areas and not so near the city of Hanoi.

I sighed with relief as the driver pulled up and stopped in front of the hotel. We had somehow made it without hitting someone or something!

Zoom took care of check-in and then carried my backpack up to the room. My room was not only large and clean but also contained amenities I did not expect. It was furnished with a television, telephone, and a small refrigerator. There were two full beds with mosquito nets, a chest, and a small table. The bathroom was very large, with a tub and shower. It contained a regular commode, not like the ones in Japan.

Before leaving to freshen up for dinner, Zoom handed me a neatly typed copy of the itinerary. I was relieved as I had heard very little of what he said as we drove along. I had been to busy "helping" the driver dodge the many obstacles on the road as I gasped at the activity and digested the reality of being in Vietnam.

Dinner that night was at a small, local, outdoor restaurant. None of these restaurants seemed to have names. I asked Zoom to choose for me, asking only that it be without meat. He returned to our small sidewalk table with a large bowl of soup for each of us. It was very tasty and just enough, as all the excitement had taken my appetite away.

We talked as we ate. Zoom told me about himself. He was thirty-four at the time, the same age as my oldest daughter. He and his wife had just had their first child, a son, born only a few days before my arrival. He told me a little about how things had been during the war. The bombing was a horrible nightmare experience for him. He lost his grandparents, who lost their lives trying to save the lives of his immediate family. By some miracle, his life and the lives of his parents and his siblings had been spared. I felt a shiver go through my body as I visualized Zoom as a small boy living through all that horror. Had bombs from my husband's plane killed his relatives? I shuddered at the thought.

A close bond was forged between Zoom and me that night.

The next few days were filled with meeting people and seeing Vietnam. I met the Deputy Director of Foreign Affairs, Zoom's big boss. He was a gracious host and invited me to be his guest for dinner that evening.

I met with Lt. Colonel John Cray, the commander in charge of the Task Force for men still missing in Vietnam. We talked at length about the circumstances of my husband's loss and about the rapport being formed between the United States detachment in Hanoi and the Vietnamese people. He felt a trust was being formed and with this trust, a greater possibility for the release of information from the Vietnam government.

My guide and now new friend, Zoom, took me to the Hanoi Army Museum. It was very depressing for me to see all the war paraphernalia. The worst exhibit for me was of Lt. Alvarez, the first American to be shot down and taken prisoner in the Vietnam war. There was a large photograph of him being taken prisoner and pieces of his airplane and his helmet, among other things.

As we left the large museum, Zoom and I looked at each other. Our eyes were filled with tears. We had both been deeply hurt by the effects of that war.

We drove to Haiphong. What a drive! Two hours on those narrow roads was a bit unnerving. I said a silent prayer and left the driver to his duty of avoiding people, animals, and carts. I turned my attention to the scenery. The countryside was beautiful; lush green, with small rolling hills. Along the roads and in the fields I could see huge water buffalo pulling carts, and small children helping the adults work in the fields. I asked the driver to stop periodically for photo shots.

Visiting Haiphong was my main reason for coming to Vietnam. It is the area in which my husband was then believed to have been shot down. (Later I received information that leads me to believe that Mike was not shot down over Haiphong Harbor, but over land.) My desire for going to Haiphong Harbor was to say a formal and final farewell to Mike, and our short life together as husband and wife. I wanted to float two red roses in the water of the harbor as a symbol of our love. This was my way of saying good-bye on Vietnamese soil where he had lost his life.

Before my private ceremony, Zoom informed me that the Director of External Affairs in Haiphong and the staff of the Joint Task Force for the search of missing men wanted to meet me. The director told me they were familiar with my husband's case and that they were doing all they could, which was not a lot as he had gone down over water. The staff was introduced. Each of them talked about how it was during the war. They would have been young men in their twenties, my age then, during that conflict.

During a break in conversation, the director invited us to join them for lunch. I looked at Zoom and he nodded an affirmative. As we walked into the dining room Zoom whispered in my ear, "This invitation is quite a surprise and a great honor."

I was treated as royalty during lunch. A gentleman on my right placed a napkin in my lap, while the one on my left served generous amounts of boiled fish, steamed prawns, potatoes, and vegetables; he even peeled the shrimp for me! Their attempts to make me feel comfortable and welcome worked wonders. I felt like a queen!

During lunch they discussed their eagerness for the United States to remove the economic boycott with their country and to let bygones be bygones.

I suggested that the reason behind the boycott was the many men who were still unaccounted for during the war in their country. They expressed sympathy for our desires but talked again of the importance of the future being the focus and letting go of the past. I related somewhat to that. That was why I was there, to let go of the past and go forward.

As we were leaving, I shook hands with the Director. He said he knew of my request to pay a special tribute to my husband. He appointed his assistant as an escort to find the perfect place at the harbor in which to float the roses.

We stopped at one of the many outdoor flower shops to purchase the roses. Then the assistant decided that if I was going to float flowers, I needed a boat. For about half an hour we drove from shop to shop in search of a boat. Finally, at a small shop, the owner showed us a boat made from colorful paper. It was about a foot-and-a-half long and a foot tall. I knew it was too tall and would never float. But this kind man was so excited that he had found a boat for me, I did not have the heart to tell him it would not work.

I paid the clerk and we were off, bound for the harbor with flowers and boat in hand.

When the perfect spot was found, Zoom parked the car and the two men guided me to the shores of Haiphong Harbor. Tears welled up in my eyes. This is where life had ended for a young man of thirty-five, with a young wife and three small daughters left behind to mourn. Now, twenty-seven years later, I was standing there to say a formal farewell to my beloved.

The two men left me alone to say what I needed to say in private. I placed the two red roses in the boat, along with a ring I had brought for the occasion, and tried to send the boat out to sea. The wind was blowing and the top-heavy boat would not sail.

Seeing my difficulty, the assistant rushed to my side to help. In his frustration to launch the boat, he took off his shoes and socks and rolled up his pants and walked the boat farther out in the water. It sailed for only a moment then capsized. He tried a few more times and finally it was obvious to us all that the wind was too strong and the boat too tall. His attempts to right the boat failed. Wet and muddy, the man gave up. I could tell the Assistant Director felt as though he had failed, even though I assured him that was all right. In my heart, I truly felt the mission had been accomplished.

The next day I told Zoom to take time off to be with his wife and newborn son. I wanted to be by myself.

I walked along the streets of Hanoi, seeing the sights and experiencing the people. Being very blond and light-skinned, I stood out like a pink panda in a herd of zebra. An uncomfortable presence was the beggars. One old lady came up to me and poked her hand in my face for a handout. Then she angrily pointed to her missing leg. A little boy stuck out his hand and he had no fingers. I felt sick to my stomach and somewhat responsible. I moved quickly from that area.

Generally speaking, I found the Vietnamese people, especially the children, very friendly. The smiles on their faces made me believe they were happy in their lives. They used their only English phrase, "Hello, Madam," over and over again. Those bright smiles on their young lovely faces touched my heart.

Zoom and I went shopping and in the evening, to a water puppet performance. Water puppetry is an art form unique to Vietnam. At that time this type of puppet show could be seen only in Hanoi. It is a spectacular show of colorful puppets skimming the water and interesting-sounding musical instruments accompanying their actions.

The morning I was to leave Hanoi, the Director of Foreign Affairs requested I stop in to say good-bye. When I arrived, he presented me with a gift, a Buddha carved from oxen bone. I had admired it when Zoom and I were shopping the day before. I was touched by his thoughtfulness.

As I left Vietnam I felt a peacefulness deep within. I no longer felt anger or resentment toward the country or its people. That was all gone and replaced with an appreciation of the beauty of the country, and gratitude for the love and understanding I received from these people whom I once thought of as my enemies. I think some of the street people thought of me as an enemy, because Americans had bombed their city. Hopefully, many of them have forgiven America by now.

Circumstances have still not been resolved concerning the loss of my late husband. They may never be, but I am now enjoying life, free of bitterness. I left Vietnam with love and respect in my heart for this small, simple country and its beautiful people.

I would like to return and see more of this beautiful country, Vietnam. It is still on my bucket list.

Northern Thailand

With Vietnam behind me I flew to Bangkok and boarded an all-night train to Chaing Mai, a city 450 miles north. I was now ready for fun.

At the train station in Chaing Mai I scanned my *Lonely Planet* guide book for accommodations. The guide book mentioned the popularity of small, privately-owned hotels know as guest houses. I selected the Chaing Moi Guest House. The owner, a lovely Thai woman, a retired English teacher, booked a trekking (hiking) trip into the mountains for me. We would be sleeping in the villages of the primitive Hills People. I was happy to learn that I could leave my large backpack with her.

On the trek was Mike, a young man from New Zealand, and Elka, Hans, and their daughter Joy, from Holland. Also joining us were Eve and Mick, a honeymooning couple from Australia. Two male Thai guides rounded out the group.

The first day was quite strenuous. I was not in the best physical shape for the steep up-and-down terrain. Zwat, one of the guides, was near my age and in great physical shape; he noticed my difficulty and insisted on carrying my small backpack. On this difficult terrain, it felt as though it weighed a ton, as I was carrying two quarts of water in it.

Four hours later, huffing and puffing and soaked with perspiration, we arrived at Karen Village. Our guides set up camp at the edge of the river. As evening approached, we became chilled from the cool mountain air, and changed from our sweat-dampened clothing into something dry.

The villagers came out to greet us in hopes we would buy their handmade wares. Their inventory consisted of bracelets, purses, hair barrettes, and colorful skirts and vests. While we shopped, talked to the villagers, and rested, our guides busied themselves with making a fire and cutting up vegetables for dinner.

We ate a delightful meal of boiled vegetables served over noodles accompanied by a spicy sauce and bread. For dessert, we were served fresh bananas the guides picked along the way. Candlelight enhanced the feeling of adventure.

After dinner, we sat around the camp fire singing songs with another group of trekkers. Then we watched while their guide played games of magic. By 9:00 we were all eager for bed.

Our bedroom was one long hut with straw mats placed side by side. The covered space was about eighteen inches above the ground with a wooden floor. We were given pillows that felt as hard as rocks and a blanket for each of us. Luckily, I brought a small blow-up pillow in my backpack. In this remote area there is no electricity or water. Our toilet was behind any tree we cared to use. As tired as I was, I did not sleep well. The wooden floor and the thin mat were hard and uncomfortable.

At 5:00 the next morning the roosters began crowing. Time to get up. As I crawled out of the hut, I saw the sun smiling an invitation to another scorching day.

The agenda for this day included a ride through the jungle on the back of an elephant, then a cruise down the river on rafts. I didn't ask what else. I was afraid the answer might be another four-hour trek!

Shortly after breakfast, the young boys of the village brought their elephants down to the river to bathe. The purpose of the baths is to remove ticks. Seeing the rapport these twelve or thir-teen-year-old boys had with their elephants was inspiring. Our guides told us these boys are presented with young elephants when the boys are about five years old. The two grow up together.

When the elephants were clean and dry, we climbed up a ladder onto a platform, then into a wooden seat strapped to the elephant's back. There were two of us per elephant. My partner was Joy, the young woman from Holland.

The grace and strength with which the elephants went up and down the difficult terrain was amazing. I felt very secure as the elephant zigzagged back and forth across the river. As we trudged across the river, I caught a glimpse of our guides cruising along the water on the handmade bamboo rafts they had constructed that morning.

What a glorious experience. Imagine. Riding an elephant through the jungle! At the end of the journey the elephants gracefully knelt, allowing us to dismount from our wooden seats. We walked a short distance to a thatched-roof hut overlooking the river, with a lovely view. Our lunch consisted of fried rice, vegetables, and fresh pineapple for dessert.

After lunch we boarded the rafts, five on one and four on the other. Our packs were securely fastened to a pole in the middle.

The trip down the river was scenic and exciting. Watching the guides expertly maneuver the rafts between rocks and sometimes through very rough rapids was breathtaking. The cruise lasted about an an hour and a half. Once back on land, we staggered a moment, trying to reclaim our land legs.

After trekking for close to an hour, we were at the Akha Village, where we spent our second night. No river here, but the village was on a plateau with lovely foliage and a mild, soothing breeze.

The villagers came to sell their crafts, but then they lingered. Some knew a few words of English but mainly the conversation was in gestures or just warm, friendly smiles. The family from Holland came prepared with gifts they brought from home. After they gave out a few little toys, the word spread and all the children flocked around us. One little girl, about two years old, caught my eye. She had enormous, sparkling black eyes with hair to match. Her bangs, resting on her little forehead, were damp from the hot, humid day. When she smiled at me, my heart did a flip. She was so precious I wanted to pick her up and take her home with me.

In Thailand, massages are extremely popular with westerners. Fellow travelers in the guest house in Chaing Mai suggested I treat myself to one. When I met one of the ladies in the village who was trained as a masseuse, (the politically correct name is now massage therapist), I jumped at the chance. My body really needed attention after the previous day's trek.

The masseuse's technique was different from what I've experienced in the United States but I enjoyed her style, until she reached my thighs. I let out a yelp and she chuckled and proceeded very gently. While she massaged, Joy and her Mom, Elka, came to watch. They had never experienced a massage nor had they seen one given. At home, the usual fee in the '90s was about $55.00 to $60.00 for an hour and a half and this lady charged about US$12 for the same length of time. Fees would certainly be different today.

After another delicious dinner of rice, vegetables, and fresh fruit, we gathered around the campfire again. This time it wasn't just us trekkers, it was mostly the villagers. One young Thai man kept us laughing. Even though we didn't know what he was saying most of the time, his antics were hysterical. I slept surprisingly well the second night with just a mat between me and the hard floor and my own pillow.

As we gathered our things together the next morning, the village children came to say good-bye, their little faces aglow with the simple delight of being alive. By our standards they live primitively, but the light in the eyes of these children radiates love and contentment. This is home and they are happy.

Spending time with the Hills People in their village was a rare, wonderful experience. I felt a little sad as we left for our final trek to transportation taking us back to Chaing Mai.

Before leaving the area, I traveled farther north to the town of Chaing Sean on the banks of the Mekong River, eleven miles from the famous Golden Triangle. This is where Burma, Laos and Thailand meet. It had a lovely view, but not much else. This was an easy day trip.

Back in Chaing Mai, I booked a reservation at the Cultural Center for dinner and to watch Thai dancers. The Thai women are incredibly beautiful, and wear their fingernails extremely long, which enhances the long line of their arms and their elegant costumes and graceful dances. The evening was enjoyable and well worth $18, even though it proved to be a tourist extravaganza.

I had many wonderful experiences in Northern Thailand, but the memory of my trek in the jungle and staying with the Hills People in their villages still lingers. I was with them only three days and two nights, but it was the highlight of my stay in the north.

Southern Thailand
– The Islands –

The train from Bangkok arrived at the busy port of Surat Thani at 6:00 in the morning. Surat Thani is mainly a jumping-off place for travelers going to the islands of Koh Samui and Koh Phangan.

When I left the train, buses were waiting to take us to the dock for a ferry to our island of choice. I purchased a ticket for Koh Samui. Allowing time for breakfast, I ordered a typical Thai meal of fried rice and vegetables.

I learned from fellow travelers that a bungalow rather than a hotel is the most popular place to stay and the least expensive. I was also told that the northern part of the island is quieter and less populated. After those busy days in northern Thailand, I felt like kicking back for a few days and the north part of the island sounded inviting.

On the two-and-one-half-hour ferry ride to the island of Koh Samui, there were vendors aboard with information about places to stay. After talking to a few of them, I chose Mae Nam beach because of the attractive photos and the write-up about the Sunrise Village Bungalows.

At the end of a beautiful cruise, we arrived at Na Thon, the small harbor for the ferry boats. Four of us piled into the back of a pick-up truck, our "taxi" to the beach. In about ten minutes we pulled off the road into a grove of palm trees and a few minutes later stopped in front of a cluster of neatly groomed bungalows. My private bungalow consisted of a small room with a full bed, a dresser, a lamp, a closet, and a bathroom with shower. A fan hung from the ceiling to ward off the heat. The cost? Can you believe this? US$3.16.

Quickly I changed into my bathing suit. Looking strange with my "farmer's tan", brown only on my arms and legs, I walked to the beach. I stopped and let out a gasp at the breathtaking sight; before me stretched a long, white, sandy beach edging clear, beautiful blue water. Palm trees were swaying in the breeze, offering protection from the extreme heat of the sun.

I threw my things on the white sand and ran into the warm, salty water of the Gulf of Thailand. I felt my body relax. I had found paradise!

After cooling off, I sat under a palm tree to watch a young couple and a man about my age play Frisbee. "Probably a man on vacation with his kids," I thought. Later I learned they were just friends. The young couple, Kathy and Russ, were from New Zealand, and Peter was from England. The four of us spent the rest of the day together. They invited me to join them for dinner that evening.

One of the major benefits of traveling alone is the opportunity to meet people. Some of those brief encounters end up being long-term relationships. As a lone traveler, you may choose to join others you meet or, if you'd rather spend time alone, you can choose that. I chose both on this trip and had memorable experiences both ways.

After a few days on the northern part of the island with my new friends, we all went our separate ways. Peter continued on his six-month trip; his next stop was Australia. Kathy and Russ were off to London to work for a few months so they could continue to finance their travels. Peter and I exchanged addresses. I promised to call him when I reached London.

I decided to go around the island to the south beaches. The day after I arrived, it began to rain. I took a ferry over to the island of Koh Phangan and it continued to rain. Rumor had it that the west coast of Thailand was dry. I took the ferry back to Surat Thani and then a bus west.

I arrived in the west coast town of Krabi in the pouring rain and found a budget hotel for the night. The room was simple, with only a bed, a small table, and a ceiling fan. The bathroom was down the hall; I shared it with others on the floor. I slept soundly in the comfortable bed. The next morning the sun was shining brightly!

I boarded a boat to the Island of Koh Phi Phi (called Pee Pee by the locals) and stayed in the Paradise Pearl Bungalows, about fifty feet from the water. My bungalow was furnished with a bed, a dresser, and bedside table with a lamp. I had a private bath and shower. This island is known for marvelous snorkeling because the water is crystal clear and colorful fish are seen brazenly close to the shore. All this for US$5.70.

As I lay in the sun on the beach I realized it was Thanksgiving Day. That evening I ate my Thanksgiving dinner alone, rice and vegetables, feeling sad and lonely, thinking of my three daughters. They were all together in Idaho at the home of Jane, my middle daughter.

The next day was actually Thanksgiving Day in the United States. There is a 15 to 16 hour time difference from Thailand to the west coast of the United States. I called Idaho, collect, and talked to all three of my daughters. They all sounded so happy and excited about being together. I hung up and felt worse!

Realizing I could choose to stay unhappy or I could do something fun, I chose to book an all-day trip to explore another small island and go snorkeling.

There were seven of us on the boat, plus the driver. The day started out sunny, but by mid-day, it began to rain and then the wind came up. I have never been comfortable on the water when it is rough and now it was getting rough. We were all soaked. No one seemed to mind when the captain said, "This is a good place to go snorkeling," and dropped the anchor.

Everyone else was laughing with glee as they strapped on their masks, snorkels and fins. I sat there a few more seconds and said to myself, "*Feel the Fear and Do It Anyway!*" I knew that if I stayed on the rocking boat I would become seasick, so I quickly put on my mask, snorkel, and fins and jumped in.

Once in the bay I felt myself relax as the dark blue liquid gently massaged my body. I ducked my head and saw so many fascinating, colorful fish that I completely forgot my fear and the rolling of the rough water. The sight beneath me released all the pent-up tension. I had a glorious time. However, getting back into the boat was a bit of a task. With the help of the captain, and a boost from a couple of the fellows from behind, up I went.

At the end of the day, I was pleased that I had overcome my fear one more time. Conquering that fear allowed me to enjoy incredible underwater scenery and to meet some adventurous new friends. During the rest of my stay on Koh Pee Pee, anytime I went into the dining room there were friendly, smiling faces and hands waving to me to join them.

I arrived in Thailand a stranger. Now, thirty days later, I was leaving with a feeling of being part of this warm, friendly country. I enjoyed Thailand; its mountains, its beaches, and its people. I was comfortable traveling now and excited about going on to another country and another culture. Instead of traveling back to Bangkok and taking a flight directly to Singapore, I chose to venture out on my own through Malaysia to reach Singapore.

Malaysia

I traveled with an international group of ten people by mini-bus from Hay Yai, Thailand, to Malaysia. This mode of transportation was the most expedient way to get through customs. The bus driver collected our passports and had them checked and stamped. We each paid him a few dollars for this service, then we walked across the border with our luggage and met the minibus on the Malaysia side. Our first stop in this country was Butterworth, to let off two of the passengers. The rest of us were continuing on to Penang. The minibus boarded a ferry to cross the Meleka Straits to Penang Island.

The driver drove us to an area of budget hotels. When I left the bus I saw a sign for the Tye Ann Hotel across the street. It had been recommended in my guide book. I picked up my backpack and walked across the street with a couple from Australia who had been on the bus. The manager said there was one bed left, in a four-bed dorm. I grabbed it. The Australian couple said good-bye and walked on to find another hotel.

While traveling, it was rare for me to make a reservation in advance. I showed up in a city and checked my guide book and called to see if they had a room or, as in this case, if it was near my transportation, I just walked in. I felt comfortable in Malaysia immediately with its wide variety of people, Malaysians, Chinese, Indians, and westerners making their home in Malaysia. Even the architecture is a conglomeration of different cultures.

The first afternoon in Penang, I was busy taking photographs when I heard a male voice from behind me say, "You can get a better view inside the walls." I turned to face a tall, slim, dark-skinned Indian man. I explained I was interested in a certain angle because of the light from the sun on the wall. I walked on and he fell in step beside me, saying with a slight accent, "Do you mind if I walk with you?" I hesitated a moment then replied, "No, I don't mind." We walked and talked. His name was Raja and he was 37 years old at the time, born in May as I was. He was born and raised in Malaysia but not Penang. He was a pleasant man and I felt comfortable with him. He suggested we visit an old English cemetery to see the tomb of Francis Light, the man who discovered Penang. I agreed to accompany him to this historical site. When it was time to return to my hotel, Raja escorted me. I thanked him for a wonderful tour and he said, "I'll be back at 8:00 this evening to take you for coffee." I was so surprised I heard myself say, "Okay," but added, "Let's make it 8:30." I didn't want to appear too eager.

Raja was late for our rendezvous. I was just beginning to think he wasn't coming when he appeared. He was most apologetic. A block from the hotel, he said, "Wait right here." He disappeared around the corner, returning shortly with a beautiful red rose for me.

After tea we walked to the harbor, sat on the sea wall and talked. Raja told me he had taken the next day off work and would like very much to show me some of the sights of Penang, if I would allow him. I was honored. He was a perfect gentleman all evening.

The four days I spent in Penang I saw Raja often. We walked, talked, and laughed a lot. It was special being escorted to all the sights by a local.

One evening we went to an Indian restaurant. I ordered rice and shrimp and Raja chose rice and mutton. As I picked up my fork to take a bite, I glanced across the table. Raja was scooping up his food with his fingers and putting it into his mouth. Then I remembered that Indians eat without utensils. I chuckled as I wondered, "What would my daughters think if I brought this dear, gentle, Indian man home for dinner?"

After dinner, we walked to the waterfront and sat on the wall. A pleasant breeze blew gently from across the water. As we talked, Raja took a small bag from his pocket. Bending down, he fastened a lovely ankle bracelet around my left ankle, saying, "As you continue on your travels, know that a tall Indian man will be thinking of you."

My last night in Penang, I met Raja after work. We went to a sidewalk cafe for tea. There I gave him a little key made of mother-of-pearl. I had purchased a number of them in San Diego to give to my Servas hosts; a key to symbolize world peace. I placed it around his neck. He thanked me and he removed a chain from around his neck. Attached to the chain was a small Buddha charm. He said he had worn it for years, never taking it off, and he wanted me to have it. I tried to object, but he insisted.

At 10:00 that evening, my bus to the Cameron Highlands arrived. Raja and I said good-bye in the pouring rain, promising to stay in touch.

I sent postcards to him as I traveled on. When I arrived home, there was a long letter waiting. He never forgot a special holiday or my birthday. He even telephoned once in a while. My friendship with Raja was one of mutual fondness and respect. We kept in touch for a number of years, then lost contact with each other.

The Cameron Highlands were a wonderful, refreshing change from the heat of Penang. It was pleasant during the day and rather chilly in the evening. The blanket they provided was certainly needed. I stayed in a private room at the Twin Pines Chalet, for about US$10. I needed a rest from dorm living for a few days.

People were friendly in the highlands. A group of us hiked together, had dinner, and played games on the porch in the evenings. A young English couple taught me how to make bracelets from embroidery thread. A man from the United States sketched a portrait of me and gave it to me as a gift.

Hazel, a lady from England, joined our group. We discovered we were both going on to Singapore and then to Bali. It was mid-December and both Hazel and I wanted a travel-mate for the holidays. We made plans to meet in Singapore and then travel to Bali together.

Our group in the Cameron Highlands had such fun together that it was not easy to say good-bye. We were all heading in different directions, but Hazel and I knew we would meet in Singapore.

Alone once again, I took a bus down the mountain and on to Melaka. I stayed at the Oriental Heritage in a dorm. Melaka (Malacca) is a picturesque old city-state. They did not have any high-rise buildings. The architecture was simple in some areas and rather ornate in others. I walked and explored, taking several photographs.

I found an international telephone and placed a call to the United States to check in with one of my daughters. "Mom's fine, having a wonderful time, will call again next week."

I promised my daughters I would call home once a week to let them know I was all right. They had no way of reaching me so I didn't want them to worry. I called each one in turn and they passed the word that mom had checked in that week. In those days I used telephone cards. It was the best way to make an international call. It was cheaper and faster. We talked about the important things instead of just chatting. When your card runs out you have to hang up. Thank God, we have e-mail and texting to keep in touch with our loved ones and friends today.

In Melaka, Stanley, the manager of the Oriental Heritage, played the guitar and sang in the bar in the evenings. During the day he taught classes in painting batiks on silk. I joined one of his classes. Not being an artist, I asked Stanley for help to draw the design. Once the design is on the silk, Stanley outlines it with hot wax. The hot wax is to keep the colors from running together. When the wax was dry, he showed me the correct way to stroke with the brush when working on cloth. Then I was on my own.

After I painted the colors on the silk, Stanley completed the rest of the process. I could see the mistakes in my work when it was finished, but Stanley said that is how you know a piece is an original. If there are no mistakes, it is probably machine made.

By now I had been traveling for almost three months; the past six weeks I had been in third-world countries. Before continuing on in third-world countries, I was going to Singapore to enjoy a much-needed rest in a modern city.

Singapore

On the bus from Melaka, Malaysia to Singapore, I sat next to a girl from Toronto, Canada. Lucky for me she had been to Singapore before so she knew her way around the city. When I told her where I was staying, she was able to give me perfect directions to get there.

Hazel and I had made plans before parting ways in the Cameron Highlands, to meet at the Waffles Homestay in Singapore. If it was full we agreed to leave a message there for each other.

The Waffles Homestay on North Bridge Street is a small hotel near everything in the city. I booked a private room for US$11.50. It was small and simple, with a window overlooking a courtyard. I checked to see if Hazel had arrived or left a message. She had not. I wrote a note for her and left it at the front desk. Then I picked up a few brochures and went out to explore Singapore.

One of the brochures was about the all-day trolley tour to the many colorful highlights of Singapore. You could get off when you wanted and then get back on and ride until you completed the entire tour. I continued exploring Singapore, picking up a free map of the city at the tourist office.

Walking in Singapore was comfortable and pleasant. The air and the city were very clean, and everyone spoke English. I ate lunch at an Italian restaurant by the canal and splurged. I ordered seafood pasta and a fresh green salad. The bill came to about US$13, more than my hotel room. The street was named «Quay Road.» It was fun having lunch on a road with my same first name.

I returned to the hotel in the late afternoon. The hot, humid day prompted me to rush to the shower to cool off. Which took no time at all because there was no hot water!

Since leaving Hong Kong I was accustomed to taking cold showers. Most of the places in which I stayed did not have hot water. But in modern Singapore, the cold water came as a shock. However, once I was wet, the cool water was refreshing.

After showering I learned that Hazel had checked in. I found her at the rooftop coffee shop of the Homestay. Over tea we discussed plans for our two days in Singapore.

That evening we walked to the Raffles department store, which displayed elegantly lighted Christmas scenes. Every hour the lighted display seemed to come alive with movement of song and dance. It was spectacular!

For the first time, the impact of how close it was to the holidays hit me. I would not be with my family and I would miss my only grandchild's first Christmas. On December 18 she would be ten months old. A feeling of nostalgia rushed over me.

The next day Hazel and I purchased an all-day ticket on the trolley. Our first stop was the Botanical Gardens. A number of wedding parties were taking advantage of these elegant gardens for their wedding pictures.

We stopped off in Chinatown where we purchased Singapore t-shirts. Hazel purchased a frilly nightgown (after Bali she was going on to Australia to meet her boyfriend). I could envision Hazel in the nightgown.

After shopping we chose an outside cafe for lunch. The proprietor seated us and suggested a bowl of Chinese noodle soup. The bowl was filled with large rice noodles and generous pieces of chicken; it was spiced perfectly. We were pleased that we had followed his suggestion because the soup was excellent.

Our next trolley stop was Sentosa. We took a cable car across the harbor to reach the island and enjoyed a nice view of the sparkling blue water below and a smattering of other small islands. But upon arrival we found it very commercial.

During the Christmas season in Singapore, the establishments go all out. Every shopping center, department store, and large hotel exhibit elaborate decorations. There was a contest and a prize would be awarded for the best display. The city was alive in the evening as the lights glimmered and sparkled, filling one's heart with the excitement of Christmas.

That evening Hazel and I went with some girls from our hotel to the famous Long Bar in the exclusive Raffles Hotel. The five of us walked into the upscale bar as though we owned the place. The other customers were not aware of our staying in a budget hotel and being able to afford only one drink.

We found a table with only four chairs. Noticing a man sitting alone, I asked if we could use one of his chairs. He smiled and nodded in affirmation.

I pulled the chair over, sat down, and said to our group, "He looks lonely. Why don't we ask him to join us?" They agreed. I extended the invitation and he was delighted.

The Long Bar is known for its Singapore Slings. When the waitress arrived, we ordered five, one of which was virgin for me. The gentleman ordered a beer.

Walter was from Australia. He was in Singapore for a few days on business. As we finished our drinks he ordered another round saying this one was on him. We graciously accepted! When the check arrived we found the Singapore Slings were $14 each and my virgin was $10! Our budgets were stretched, and this was before dinner.

As we rose to leave, someone asked Walter if he would like to join us for dinner. He smiled from ear to ear and said, "Yes."

A couple of the girls knew of an outdoor garden restaurant that served fresh broiled fish. The prices were rather inexpensive by Singapore standards and therefor it was a popular place. We told Walter our plans and he was delighted to remain with us.

During the ten-minute walk to the restaurant, Walter told us that he was staying at the Raffles Hotel. The Raffles is the most expensive hotel in Singapore! This was our first clue that he was a well-to-do businessman. Dinner with us might be a come-down from his normal manner of dining, but judging by the smile on his face, he was enjoying himself.

I think he learned from our conversations that we were budget travelers. When the check came, he insisted on paying for all of our dinners.

Later, saying good-bye to Walter, we thanked him for his generosity. He said with a smile on his face, "The pleasure was mine. I travel a lot and most evenings I have a drink and then dine alone. Spending the evening with you lovely ladies has been delightful."

Indonesia

Hazel and I departed Singapore on different flights, planning to meet on Kuta Beach on the Island of Bali. From the airport at Despensar, I went to the American Express office located at Sanur Beach, a few miles from Kuta Beach. I was expecting a package from my daughters. After claiming my package, I took a taxi to Kuta Beach. I heard for years about the beautiful sunsets at Kuta Beach on the Island of Bali. I was eager to see this much-talked-about scene for myself.

The driver dropped me off at the Three Sisters Hotel in the adjoining beach town of Legian. No vacancies. A note from Hazel was waiting for me. She had checked into the Legian Beach Bungalows next door where she had booked a room for us. The clerk gave me a key. The room was quite large—twin beds and a large private bath with a shower. There was a little front porch with two comfortable chairs separated by a table. The price of the room was about US$6 each.

Hazel was out so I took this opportunity to open my mail. Letters from home! It was so good hearing from my daughters. I opened a package from my daughter Jane. Books, a t-shirt from the film she had just completed, a pair of dangling earrings, and a cute Christmas tree ornament photo of me, my daughter Kathy and my granddaughter Clara, taken at her christening, before I left California. I felt homesick and disappointed there wasn't more. I wanted more mail!

Hazel had not returned so I walked down to the beach. Here, I felt more disappointment. All the stories made Bali sound so extraordinary but it was just another beach with white sand and blue water. I expected crowds of people but it was quiet. I was in the mood for lots of people and festivities. After all, it was the holiday season.

After an hour on the beach, I walked back to the room. Before I got into feeling too sorry for myself, Hazel returned to the room. Just having a friend to talk with was a tremendous help in getting past the feelings of loneliness. Hazel is a kindhearted, gentle woman with a ready smile. She was about ten years younger than I, with a daughter and a son in their twenties. We were glad to have each other during the holidays.

Before I left Idaho, my friend Steven told me he would be vacationing in Bali during the time I planned to be there. He gave me a contact number. I called and left a message with my name and the telephone number of my hotel. Later that day, Steven stopped by the hotel, looking tanned and healthy. He was obviously enjoying his vacation at Legian and Kuta Beaches. He had been going to the same area for the past nine years, staying a month or six weeks.

Steven invited me to a dinner party in his honor. He would be leaving soon to return to the United States. His farewell party was being held at a lady friend's home on the island, about a 15-minute drive. As we approached the home I could see it was large, but a high fence made it impossible to tell anything else about the structure.

Inside the gate, the grounds were illuminated with colored lights. Small lily ponds were stationed throughout the large estate, with bridges crossing to the entrance of the house. Lustrous green foliage and colorful flowers grew everywhere.

The house itself was three stories, with high ceilings, giving it an open, spacious look. Suspended from the ceiling were large fans to keep the air circulating. Mimi, our hostess, asked Steven to take me on a tour of her home. I was very impressed with her tasteful eye in decorating. The furnishings were elaborate but kept in the flare of island living.

Mimi is a beautiful Balinese woman of Chinese decent. She was gracious and friendly as she welcomed us into her home. She introduced her brother-in-law, our cook for the evening. He greeted us, then excused himself to return to his creations in the kitchen.

The meal was outstanding. It consisted of five or six courses. We started with an omelet smothered in a tasty sauce. Next came chicken wings and a tofu-vegetable dish in a somewhat spicy sauce.

I had seconds of everything. Then the main course was served!

The main course of white fish was creatively arranged on a colorful platter with a crispy crumb-like topping. I accepted a serving of the fish, even though I was filled to the brim from eating all the other delectable, mouth-watering dishes. After this feast, tea was served, followed by a piece of cheesecake. I ate that, too!

The next day, suffering from a food "hangover" from over-indulgence, I spent a couple of hours on the beach with Hazel. Any longer in the hot island sun would have resulted in a sunburn. With our sun quota for the day used up, we decided to go shopping.

Shopping became quite irritating very soon. The vendors with watches were the worst. They'd see a tourist and would stick their wooden boxes right in your face. Getting around them was next to impossible. They did not listen to a polite "no" so we had to be rude. Shopping was not a pleasant experience at the beaches.

That afternoon Hazel received a telephone call from her boyfriend. He called with the sad news that her best friend was in the hospital. Her cancer had worsened and she might not recover.

Hazel decided to go home to be with her friend. She called the airlines and the first flight she could take back to London was on December 20, five days away.

Having a few days before her departure we decided to go to Ubud, about a two-hour bus ride from the beach. It is known as the artist colony in the mountains. I didn't feel as though we had gained altitude, but the temperature had dropped.

In Ubud we stayed at the Puri Muwa Bungalows on Monkey Forest Road. The bungalow was quiet and comfortable and very affordable; it included breakfast.

Ubud is a unique, sprawled-out small town. It is said to be the best place to see the Balinese performing Barong dancing. My favorite was a performance by a group Balinese children. Their costumes were exquisite and their makeup colorful but tastefully applied. The young children's performance in song and dance was extremely professional. The orchestra, consisting of all Balinese instruments, added to the enchantment of the show.

Ubud had many excellent restaurants, but the Lotus Cafe was a disappointment to us. This restaurant, according to all the guide books, was a must. My book described it as, «The place to see and to be seen.» It didn't measure up to that when we were there. No one was there to see us. The place was literally empty.

I ordered fettuccine for dinner. It was not all that tasty and the price was a little high compared to the standards we had gotten used to. After eating, we walked out to the garden where there was a huge pond filled with lotus flowers and lilies, which were gently swaying in the light evening breeze. I made a mental note to return during the day to take photographs.

The more we wandered through and around Ubud, the more enchanted we became with the picturesque spot. It is truly unusual. We visited the monkey sanctuary where the small, lively monkeys ran free. We bought peanuts to feed them as we walked along, being careful not to let them bite a finger in their haste to snatch a peanut.

After wandering through the wood carvers' shops and buying small gifts for our loved ones, we stumbled upon the Panorama Restaurant on the edge of the lush green rice fields. We decided to stop for a light lunch, and ordered a vegetarian dip made with tofu and chives and a bowl of cold soup with a coconut milk base. The restaurant not only had a relaxing atmosphere, but fine food as well. While we sipped our soup we talked and listened to the tingling wind chimes dancing softly while a meditation tape played in the background. (I have found, so many times while traveling, that some of the best adventures happen accidentally).

The next day, a guided tour took us into the central part of Bali. Two other ladies were on the bus with us, one from London and one from Czechoslovakia. The driver drove past terraced rice fields where he stopped to give us time to take photographs and to admire the unusual terrain. We visited a few temples and had lunch overlooking Lake Batur and Mt. Batur.

That evening the four of us went to another Balinese Barong dance. It was performed in a little village about a half-hour's taxi drive from Ubud. The dance was not as elegant as some others Hazel and I had seen. It was more like a ceremony one might witness in a small village. I had fun talking to one of the male per-formers before the show. He gave me a flower to wear in my hair. Afterwards I took photographs of him and some of the young girls in the performance.

Back in Ubud, we went to dinner at Cafe Wayan's. It lived up to its reputation. That was the best meal we had in Ubud. And as I said before, Ubud is known for excellent restaurants.

The morning Hazel was to fly back to London, she went out for some last-minute shopping. While she was out, I walked to the transportation counter and booked a bus and ferry ticket to Lombok Island, east of Bali.

At 3:00 that afternoon Hazel and I hugged as we said good-bye. Parting was difficult, as our friendship had grown strong in the short time we had known each other. Returning to the bedside of her sick friend would not be easy for Hazel. Being alone at Christmas time would not be easy for me. With a wave of the hand and tears in our eyes we promised to keep in touch. (We are still in touch every so often. And have reunited in London and Paris twice).

I spent the rest of that afternoon getting my things in order. I took the gifts I had purchased to the packaging and shipping office to send home. I sent all my packages by surface mail as it was half the price. This did not apply to exposed film, which I air-mailed home to be processed. (Today we all have digital cameras or iPhones to take photos with.)

With a much lighter backpack, I left the next morning by shuttle bus to the ferry. I shared the van with a couple from Germany. It was only an hour's drive, but it was really hairy. The lady was so nervous, I hoped she would make it without having a heart attack. The driver drove extremely fast along the narrow, windy roads. He blew the horn, assuming the dogs, cows, and children would get out of the way. Miraculously, they did. By now I had grown accustomed to their manner of driving and most of the time I sat there rather relaxed. This insane driving began in Vietnam and never got any better. These countries do not have safety rules as we do. Right or wrong, that is just the way it is.

When we arrived at the dock, the German lady looked as though she was in shock. I shook my head, grabbed my backpack, and walked toward the huge ferry waiting to depart to Lombok Island. Four hours later we docked, and I boarded a bus to

Senggigi Beach. Scanning my guide book for a hotel, I found Pondah Senggigi. The write-up listed it as the most active hotel at the beach, and the only hotel that had evening entertainment. Now that I was alone, I wanted to be in a place with activity.

The driver waited while I ran into the office at the Pondah Senggigi to see if a room was available. One was. I paid him and checked in. My room wasn't ready so I walked to an outdoor restaurant for lunch. Two ladies and a man were the only customers. When I walked in, they looked up, smiled, and motioned for me to join them. We introduced ourselves. Sue and Jan were from Australia and John was from Ireland. After eating lunch with very pleasant company, I found that my room was ready. I thanked them for inviting me to join them. I walked away feeling that I would most likely see them again.

The room at the Pondah Senggigi was one of the nicest rooms I'd had so far. It was newly decorated with matching drapes and bedspreads. The twin beds were very comfortable. The room was located several hundred feet from the restaurant and bar so the noise of the evening was muffled.

I had dinner with John, the man I met earlier in the day. The food was good and the music mellow and soothing. Before leaving that night, the singer announced there would be a live band the next night for dancing. John was going on to another island the next day, so he didn't take note of the announcement. But I did. I was pleased because I love to dance.

I awakened the next morning to the sound of rain. By the time I finished my breakfast the sun was shining off and on. I put my bathing suit on under my shorts and stuffed a rain poncho into my beach bag. I was prepared for either rain or shine.

I walked leisurely along the uncrowded beach. Passing a few of the expensive hotels with private beaches, I had to walk into the water so as not to infringe upon private property.

Later in the day black clouds appeared. I wanted to take one last swim in the warm water before returning to the hotel. As I walked into the surf, I noticed an attractive man with gray, curly hair playing in the surf. It was difficult to gauge his age; I thought probably mid-forties. He smiled at me and made a comment about the strong undertow. A conversation ensued.

Not detecting an accent, I asked where he was from.

"Canada, the Vancouver area," he replied.

His name was Perry and he had been traveling for about three months. He hoped to be traveling for a year and a half before returning to Canada. When he discovered I was staying at the Pondah Senggigi, he said, "I hear they have the best restaurant in this area." Then he asked if I would like to meet him and his traveling companion for dinner. I told him I would be delighted. We agreed to meet between 7:30 and 8:00 p.m.

Just as I returned to my room the rains came. I turned on the water and climbed into the shower. Just then, both electricity and water went off. Thank goodness this happened before I had lathered my hair with shampoo or soaped my body.

An hour later the electricity and water were turned on and I showered and shampooed. Then I dressed in a casual sundress in tune with the atmosphere of the island.

The rain continued to fall; an umbrella was needed for the short distance to the restaurant. With this downpour I wasn't sure if my dinner companions would venture out.

I waited about ten minutes, then ordered dinner. I had eaten only fresh pineapple on the beach for lunch so I was ravenous and savored every bite of the dinner of fried noodles and shrimp. I glanced up and saw Perry and a very tall man enter the restaurant. I waved and they walked over.

Perry introduced me to his friend Bruno, from Switzerland. He was younger, probably in his early thirties, and very tall, about 6'3" or more. His hair was brown, his eyes blue, and he wore a grand smile. His English was excellent and I liked him immediately.

The two men met in Bali and had been traveling together since. They rented motorbikes while in Ubud to go into the mountains. Bruno's bike hit a rut and sent him flying. He dislocated his shoulder and was still recuperating. That is why he was not at the beach in the afternoon when I met Perry. He didn't want to be tempted to go into the water. It's too hot and humid in Indonesia to be at a beach and not go into the water to cool off!

Renting motorbikes in Thailand and on the islands in Indonesia is extremely popular because it is the best way to reach some of the remote areas where it is the most beautiful. However, as Bruno found out, it is also dangerous. The roads are narrow and everyone drives too fast. No one wears a helmet. I saw many girls with severe burns on their legs from the exhaust. I wonder if the country has more rules today compared to the early 90s?

It was a fun-filled evening with my two new male friends. I danced with Perry most of the evening. Then Bruno decided to venture out on the floor, being very cautious of his injured shoulder. His height was a blessing. Most people on the dance floor were not tall enough to jeopardize his shoulder.

As Perry and I made plans to meet at the beach late the next afternoon, Bruno said, "Let's have dinner here again tomorrow night." I was thrilled to have dinner and dance again tomorrow night with two attractive men. I said, "Yes, let's do."

It rained all day the next day. I spent most of the time reading and writing postcards in the hotel restaurant. Not a good day for the beach! I wondered if I should bother to go to the Gili Islands. In the rain, the crossing in small boats might be an unpleasant experience.

As I contemplated my dilemma, John, the man from Ireland, joined me. He was just returning from the Gili Islands. He said, "The snorkeling was brilliant." (Brilliant is an English word Europeans and down-under folks use when they really like something.)

"And," he added, "the islands are free of all motor vehicles but filled with fun, friendly people."

After talking with John, I decided that I didn't care if it was raining. If the snorkeling was brilliant, I'd be wet in the water anyway.

The Gili Islands consist of three islands off the coast of the big island of Lombok. The word Gili is literally translated as island, but they still call the little string of three islands the Gili Islands. Gili Air is the smallest and closest to the main island of Lombok.

Gili Meno is next, and a few miles farther out in the Flores Sea is Gili Trawangan, the largest of the three.

I talked with John a little more about the islands, read my Lonely Planet guide book, and decided. I chose to go to Trawangan. I put on my rain poncho and walked over to the transportation desk to make reservations for the next day. It was December 23 and I wanted to be some place fun and lively for Christmas.

That evening during dinner with Perry and Bruno, I told them my plans. Perry asked for my address in the United States so he could reach me when he returned to Canada.

The bus left Senggigi Beach at 9:00 the next morning. We drove along the coast enjoying the breathtaking view. The driver was the most cautious I had experienced since arriving in Southeast Asia. This allowed me to sit back, completely relax, and enjoy the lush scenery.

An hour later, eight of us boarded a medium-sized boat for the cruise to the islands. There were four young Balinese men to man the boat. We stopped at Gili Air first, the smallest and most primitive of the islands. There is no electricity on Gili Air, but it could be a romantic place for a honeymoon or a love affair, neither of which was for me this trip, unfortunately.

We continued on to Gili Meno, larger than Gili Air, and rather nondescript from what I could see. The last stop was Gili Trawangan. The crossing was enjoyable, with smooth water and blue, sunny skies.

The transportation on the island was by horse-drawn carts. Not knowing where I wanted to stay, I hired a young man and his cart. After a few stops I found a place I liked.

The young man carried my backpack into the room and told me how much I owed him. "5,000 rupiah, please", he said. I gave him double that amount saying, "Merry Christmas." The big smile on his face, when he saw how much I gave him, filled my heart with pleasure. The 10,000rp was equivalent to about US$2.50 I understand that the road laborers in Indonesia made less than that for a day's work back then.

There was a cool breeze from the porch of my rather large bungalow and I could see the water. It was Christmas Eve. This was a perfect place to spend Christmas. I sat in one of the chairs on the front porch to enjoy the view and the heavenly breeze. A few minutes later a young woman from the bungalow next to mine came out on her porch. She introduced herself, telling me she was from Melbourne, Australia, and invited me to join her and some friends for dinner.

Belinda and I joined Karen and David at the Boroburu Restaurant. Karen and David were from England. They suggested I order the fresh barbecued fish. They thought it was the best item on the menu. We all ordered the same dish. A short time later the restaurant was filled to capacity. When our food arrived, I knew why. On a large white platter was a whole fish that had been cooked to perfection. Inside the moist, flaky carcass was an exquisite-tasting stuffing of cornmeal, butter, and spices. The fish was served with lots of extra lemon and tartar sauce. The meal was brilliant (my new English word), and so was the price. If memory serves me right, we paid less than US$4 for that scrumptious meal.

After a long, leisurely dinner, Karen and David said good-night and returned to their room. Belinda and I went next door to Rudy's Pub. It was filled with lively people and upbeat music. We were both asked to dance immediately. Indonesian men are attracted to western women. Age seemed to be irrelevant to them. If your skin is light, the young men were very attentive.

After a few dances it was obvious that a dance partner was not needed. People got up and danced when and if they felt the urge. Sometimes only young Balinese men filled the floor. Many of them are handsome, actually beautiful. Their features are slightly delicate and feminine. Most of the younger men wore their silky, wavy black hair quite long. Their physiques were usually slim and trim.

About midnight a torrential downpour commenced. The rain did not deter the dancing. At 2:00 that morning, during a slight break in the rain, I decided to run for my bungalow. Then I discovered the electricity had been turned off. I had a flashlight with me but the batteries were dead. I made a mental note to replace them the next morning. Carrying my sandals I walked into about eight inches of water trying to find my bungalow. Somehow I made it without falling or breaking a toe!

In the room I groped around for a candle. None to be found. I gave up, reached for a towel, dried off my wet body, and fell into bed.

I slept until I heard the roosters crow. I smiled. I was getting used to that alarm clock. Anytime I was away from the larger cities, the trusty roosters were there to let me know a new day was breaking in my tiny part of the world.

It was Christmas morning, 1993. The gifts Jane sent had been opened in Bali, but there was one that I discovered in my backpack when I first arrived in Japan back in September. It was wrapped in Christmas paper. An attached note read, "DO NOT OPEN UNTIL DECEMBER 25. Love, Suzie." I carried it around for three long months!

I quickly ripped off the paper. There was a five-by-seven framed photograph of my daughter Kathy and her daughter, my precious little granddaughter, Clara, with big smiles on their faces. They seemed to be saying "Merry Christmas" to me. I was overcome with love, followed by an intense feeling of sadness and loneliness for my daughters and their families. The tears came. I allowed them to flow until there were none left.

After a good cry I felt better. I decided to take a walk around the island. The night before, my friends told me it was an easy one-and-a-half-hour walk. As I started out on my jaunt, there were still some black clouds in the sky from the rainstorm. But the morning sun was trying its best to push its orange head through those ominous clouds.

I encountered many domestic animals as I walked, especially little baby goats. They were so cute. On the beaches it was common to find goats, cows, and horses all mixed in with the sunbathers.

After an invigorating walk and a refreshing swim, I was hungry. Breakfast was included in the price of the room so I stopped by the office to tell the desk clerk I was ready to eat.

I showered quickly and sat on the porch to wait for the food. Belinda came out on her porch just as both of our breakfasts arrived. She joined me. We wished each other a Merry Christmas, and talked while we devoured the delicious banana pancakes and sipped our hot tea. I told her how much I missed my daughters and my young granddaughter, and I was happy I could spend time with her and our other friends. She missed her family too, but she did not say too much about her family. And she was happy, as I was, that we were together at Christmas.

In the afternoon, Belinda and I met Karen and David on the beach. We rented snorkels, but the water was rather murky from the heavy rains of the night before. There was also an undertow. As the undertow became stronger, we returned our snorkeling gear. Later we heard that someone had been caught in the undertow and was not found. They did not have lifeguards at the beach to rescue a swimmer who was in danger.

A group of us who had met on the beach in the afternoon gathered for dinner that evening. If we had been a party of ten we could have ordered a turkey, specially roasted for Christmas Dinner. But we were only seven, so we settled for the tasty fish dinner of the night before.

Belinda, Karen, and David told us they were going on to Kuta Beach on Lombok Island the next morning. I elected to join them as I planned to go in that direction in a couple of days anyway.

In the early morning I was awakened by the sound of rain and howling wind. The wind was blowing so hard I thought it might be the beginning of a hurricane. I had visions of my bungalow being picked up from its stilts and blown out to sea! I jumped out of bed and dressed, just in case.

At 7:00 that morning I stuck my head out the door to survey the situation and discovered Belinda all packed and ready to leave. I could not believe that the boats would actually cross in these winds. I walked over to the dock and asked a man if the boats would be leaving as scheduled. He smiled at me and said, "No problem." Surprised, I returned to my bungalow and packed.

After breakfast we walked to the dock together. I wore the rain poncho to keep myself and my backpack as dry as possible. We boarded the boat and started our journey. That was the roughest water I had ever experienced in my life. Now I knew why these young Balinese men were in such great physical shape. They had to work hard in windy weather to keep the small boats from capsizing. They were masters at keeping the vessel at the right angle in the huge waves. Many times I have wondered what possessed me to make that trip that day. I could have waited, I was not on a time schedule. Even though there were a number of scary moments, I didn't get seasick.

The surf at the shoreline was treacherous. When we reached shore, one fellow gabbed my backpack and carried it over his head in the waist-deep water. Another man picked me up and carried me to land. I was grateful for their help.

While we waited for our transportation to Kuta Beach, I purchased a t-shirt from a local vendor. I went to the toilet to change from my dripping wet clothes into a dry shirt and pulled a pair of dry shorts from my backpack to replace the soaked ones I was wearing. In the pouring rain we started our four-or-five-hour journey to Kuta Beach. Many of the vehicles were very old. This one did not have a defroster. I was the substitute that day. I sat in the front seat and wiped the mist from the windshield for the driver.

Thank God, there was a break in the rain when we arrived at Kuta Beach, Lombok. The driver pulled up in front of the Perma Shuttle Bus office to let us out. Next to the office were bungalows. Walking directly there, I accepted the first bungalow shown to me. The others ventured on in search of nicer accommodations. I just wanted to get settled and out of the rain. If they found something better I could join them the next day. An hour later they were back. The Segare Anak Bungalows, for US$3.85 per night, were by far the best that beach had to offer.

I was very pleased with my small bungalow. It had twin beds, a small dresser, and a separate toilet and shower. No hot water, but I was used to that. The small front porch had two chairs with a view of the water across the street. I could see a large, picturesque beach even though it was overcast and raining.

Later, when the rain cleared, I went out to explore my new surroundings. It was a lovely setting with large rocks along the coastline. Some of the huge rocks protruded out of the water, and people sat outside in the early evening to watch the sunset.

The locals were warm and friendly. They were not there to sell anything, just to talk and to make one welcome. It was a refreshing change from Bali and Senggigi Beach.

During walks and exploring excursions I wandered over to the bungalows next door to mine. I was still curious to compare another bungalow to the one I had. The young man in charge was one of those beautiful Balinese men. He was probably in his early twenties, tall and slim, with black wavy hair and a pair of sparkling brown eyes that were difficult not to get lost in. His radiant smile was warm and friendly. I asked to see a bungalow. He told me all the bungalows were full, but he had one available room. I agreed to inspect it. The room was dark and dreary with one window for ventilation. I thanked him and walked back to my bungalow, feeling grateful I had followed my initial instinct.

Before dinner that evening I sat on my porch reading and relaxing. It started to rain. Just as I was getting up to look for my umbrella for a quick dash to the restaurant, I saw a very tall man run past my bungalow. It looked like Bruno. Could it be?

Sure enough, when I walked into the restaurant, there sat Perry and Bruno with a group of people. When they saw me they waved me over, making room at the table. They introduced me to their friends, a couple from Sweden and a couple from Norway.

I eagerly joined in with the laughing, joking, fun group. I saw Belinda and the others come in and asked them to join us but they declined. It seemed the rain had put them in a dark mood. I didn't want gloom so I stayed with the group that chose laughter.

After dinner we all ordered banana pancakes with chocolate syrup for dessert. I was first introduced to pancakes as a dessert on the islands in Thailand. The pancakes are lighter than what we are used to, but heavier than a French crepe.

As we talked and sipped our tea, a little more quiet now after all the food, I felt a presence behind me and heard a gentle voice in my ear, "Hi, remember me?"

I turned and looked into the eyes of the gorgeous Indonesian man who had shown me the room earlier. Surprised to see him, I smiled and said, "Yes, I remember you."

Before I knew what was happening he pulled up a chair and sat beside me. With his broken English and my hearing problem, understanding him was difficult. I felt uncomfortable trying to converse with him, but I did not want to be rude by ignoring him. I tried to keep a conversation going with the others as well. It never occurred to the young man to ask if he could join us, or that he might be intruding. While traveling I learned to accept and honor the people and their different customs.

When some of his friends arrived he left our table to join them. Even though I was relieved, I must admit I was delighted by the attention from this young, handsome man.

Perry, Bruno, and their friends were leaving the next day. Perry and Bruno were traveling back to Bali to have Bruno's shoulder checked. We said good-bye, thinking maybe we would run into each other again. We didn't. I have never heard from them, but I will always have fond memories of the fun time I had with these two men on the islands of Indonesia.

The next evening I dined with Belinda, Karen, and David. It was a quiet evening. They were still in a slump. After dinner, as we sipped our tea, the young Indonesian man came in, walked right over, and sat down beside me. I couldn't remember his name, but introduced my friends to him. I felt strongly attracted to this young man. It wasn't that I didn't trust him, I didn't trust myself. Age is not an issue for the men of Indonesia, but it was for me. A twenty-one-year-old and me? I don't think so!

The next day the weather cleared. Loaded with Perry's information of the many places to explore, off Belinda, Karen, David, and I went.

Our first destination was a view area. We walked to the top of a hill to a spectacular panoramic view of the hills, villages, and the sea. We walked down the other side through farmland, being careful not to step on the plants. We reached the beach on that side of the hill and sat down to watch some boys fly fishing. They saw us and waded out of the water to sit and chat.

The others returned to the bungalows but I lingered to enjoy the remote, secluded area. The sun was getting extremely hot so I found a shade tree in a grassy area and sat down to read. After a few pages I looked up and an entire herd of cows was grazing all around me. I realized they were seeking the shade too. I left them to munch in peace and walked back to my bungalow.

Belinda, David, and Karen left that afternoon. As we exchanged addresses and said good-bye, I didn't feel sad to be left alone. I really loved and felt comfortable at Kuta Beach. Besides, there were other areas nearby that I wanted to explore.

I wanted to see Tanjung Aan Beach, about five kilometers away. It was said to be one of the most superb beaches on this end of the Lombok Island. I started my adventure early in the morning so I could beat the heat.

I strolled past farms while watching the owners work the fields, their plows being pulled by a horse or sometimes a cow. As I approached a small house, the entire family came to the roadside to say "hello". The children were eager to have me take photographs of them.

The scenery was so engaging that I walked slowly, so the five-kilometer excursion took much longer than usual. Because the day was heating up, I sat on a cement wall for a rest and took photographs of the enchanting countryside. After cooling off, I walked on toward the sandy beach area. Struck by the beauty, I reached for my camera. It wasn't there! Oh, no. My stomach took a turn and my heart skipped a beat. Where could I have lost it? Then I remembered sitting on the cement wall. I walked back in the now very hot sun. No camera! I sat down and asked the Universe to please return it to me. I always ask for help when I lose or misplace something. I feel if is supposed to remain in my possession, it will be returned. And if not, someone needs it more than I.

There was nothing else I could do. I walked back to the beach. I couldn't take photos but I could enjoy the beauty, try to relax on the sand, and cool off in the water.

After a swim in the warm, clear, blue water I walked toward the area where the tour buses congregate. As I walked along the beach I came upon a man lying on his blanket. Passing by, I spotted a camera hanging on a little branch stuck in the sand. The case looked just like mine.

I stopped and asked, "Did you find that camera?"

He looked up, smiled, and said, "Well, my buddy actually found it and left it in my care while he went surfing."

Then I remembered two men riding past me on a motor scooter as I was walking back to find my camera. He and his friend were staying at the same place as I, so I could thank the man later and maybe buy him a drink or dinner.

I had trusted, and one more time the Universe had responded to my request.

I reclaimed my camera and happily went on my way. I reached the observation point with all the tour buses. I climbed up on a large rock and once again experienced the beauty and splendor of this primitive, but incredibly charming area.

This view would not be the same much longer. I was told that there were plans for five five-star hotels to be built near Tanjung Aan in the next few years. I wonder what it looks like at that beach now? I am so grateful to have seen it in its natural splendor.

I walked back to the road and flagged down a "bemo," the local taxi. Climbing in, I noticed a few locals and a westerner. The westerner said in a French accent, "I see you found your camera." It was the man who found my camera! We met that evening so I could thank him properly by buying dinner.

I left Kuta Beach reluctantly. It had been a relaxing time with friendly people, in an area with natural, untouched beauty.

With the passing of time things change, and if I returned to this area it would never be as peaceful as it was in late 1993.

On New Year's Eve I returned to the Island of Bali, staying at Padangbai Beach right at the seaside. When I checked into a hotel, a friendly man at the desk told me about a New Year's dance that evening, and then asked if I would go with him. When I asked where it was, he said ten kilometers away. I politely declined. If the party was being held at the beach I might have gone, but I did not want to be out on the roads in Indonesia on New Year's.

So, instead of going to a party with a young (probably 25-year-old) Indonesian man, I had dinner alone in a restaurant overlooking the water. Afterwards I sat on an old tree stump by the water looking up at the star-studded sky. As I sat there, I reflected back. I had been traveling for three months. I experienced a lot of inner growth. The camera incident especially validated my belief in asking the Universe for help and direction. Then, from behind a hill, a ray of orange emerged and the moon slowly showed its face. As I sat there watching its reflection on the still water, it disappeared behind a big, black cloud.

It left a feeling, not of loneliness but of contentment. At 9:00 I returned to my room, did my toiletries and climbed into bed to read before turning off the light. Waking up later, I looked at my watch. It was 12:00 midnight. I said Happy New Year to myself. Knowing it was now January 1, 1994, I turned over and fell back asleep.

On New Year's Day the hotel posted a flyer announcing a Barong Dance to be held in the center of the small town. I walked the two short blocks to the town center and from the size of the crowd I was sure the entire town had turned out for the festivities. I found these dancers to be quite talented. The girls were beautiful and graceful with their synchronized dancing.

As I watched, a lovely Indonesian woman, nursing her small child, smiled at me and struck up a conversation. As we talked, she introduced me to her other three children, her sister, and her mother, treating me as if I were her special guest.

When the male dancers come out to perform, it is customary for the women to squat down to watch them. Being unsure about what I was supposed to do, I watched the young woman for cues as to when to stand and when to squat respectfully.

Barong dancing became much more meaningful for me that evening. It was not a stage performance for tourists; it was a religious ceremony for the residents of this small beach town. I had been lovingly included.

When the ceremony was over, the young woman said good-bye and escorted her four young ones home.

Barong is probably the best known dance in Bali. It is a storytelling dance. It is narrating the fight between good and evil. This dance is the classic example of the Balinese way of acting out mythology, resulting in myth and history being blended into one reality.

I traveled by minibus from the east coast of Bali to Lovina Beach on the north coast. Once again I passed Mt. Batur on the trip through the cool mountains. Coming down from the mountains, I could feel the hot, humid breeze. Lovina Beach is known for its black volcanic beaches, a real contrast to the white beaches. There was a relaxed, easy-going atmosphere here. Lovina Beach is a stopping-off place for travelers who enter Bali from Java or for those of us who are leaving Bali to enter Java.

I found a bungalow, only steps from the beach, which included breakfast. Again I had a very nice front porch from which to enjoy the sea breeze. I changed into my swimsuit and walked to the water's edge to read. As I opened my book, a young girl, about eleven or twelve years old, came over. She spoke a little English and I was thrilled that she came to talk, rather than to try to sell me something.

After she left, a local man in his twenties joined me. He spoke very good English and I learned he was a Barong dancer in the area. As we talked, he told me a little about the religions in Indonesia. He said Bali is primarily Hindu and Java is Muslim. He told me he had never left the island of Bali.

When I was ready to walk back to the bungalow, he asked if we could meet later for a drink. This time I told a little white lie. I said my boyfriend was waiting in my room for me.

Lovina Beach is a delightful place even with its black sand and murky water. It is a little fishing village laced with western visitors. The people are friendly and the vendors are low-key. If you say "no," they hear you. They enjoy just sitting and talking.

The days went quickly, but the evenings were slightly lonely. At the beach I was making contact with the locals, but when dinnertime came I was alone. After dinner the only thing to do was go to bed. The electrical power was so weak that the light in my room was inadequate for reading.

Next, I booked transportation to Yogyakarta on the island of Java. I had to wait until 7:00 in the evening for bus transportation. The hotel clerk said I could store my things there and I could shower before leaving.

The day of departure, during breakfast, I met Bernard from France and Damen from England. They invited me to join them to visit the Buddhist Temple and the Holy Hot Springs. Accepting the invitation, I ran quickly back to my room, finished packing my bag, gave it to the manager to store, and off we drove in their rented Suzuki.

After driving the ten kilometers to the Buddhist Temple, we agreed we had seen so many temples that the thrill was gone. The Hot Springs boasts a lush garden area and three hot tubs. Hot, medium, and perfect could be used to describe the water temperatures. Bathing suits are required. We tried all three tubs before taking a break for lunch. We ate in a quiet, open-air restaurant on the premises.

During our lunch conversation, Bernard hinted that he and Damen were more than friends. When they realized I wasn't the least bit bothered by their being gay, they relaxed.

That evening, when it was time to leave for the bus station, my two new friends insisted on driving me. I accepted gratefully as the half-mile walk in the heat with my heavy backpack was not inviting.

The very crowded bus arrived. There was no luggage compartment so the luggage was placed in the aisle. I climbed over bags and baggage and fell into a seat. The driver threw my backpack in behind me.

We arrived in Surabaya, Java, at 3:00 the following morning; then I had an hour's wait for a train to Yogyakarta. We were inland and it was hotter. No cooling sea breeze here. After a long, hot, sweaty train ride I arrived in Yogyakarta at 12:30 in the afternoon.

I checked into a dreary-looking hotel just across the street from the train station and stretched out on the hard bed. When I awakened, I went to take a shower and discovered there was not a shower, just a bucket to pour water over your body to wash off the soap. No shower. This would never do.

I went out to check a couple of other low-budget hotels nearby but they were no better. I walked into the Asia-Africa, a medium-priced hotel; it felt like heaven. I was shown to a small but nice room with a shower. The hotel even had a swimming pool. All this for a little over $10. I registered and moved. I was in the middle of the island and it was very hot and humid. Without the sea for cooling off, I considered the swimming pool a real bonus.

Yogya, (The Y is pronounced like a J) is the short version for Yogyakarta used by travelers and locals. Yogya is an easy-going city and comparatively economical for the budget traveler. It is the cultural and artistic center of Java.

I took this opportunity to go on a few of the many guided tours the tourist office offered. I visited Prambanan, the largest Hindu temple complex in Java. The outer compound contains the ruins of 224 temples, only two of which had been restored. There was a wonderful statue of Ganesh, the elephant-headed son of Shiva, and many more.

I took a bus tour to Borobudur Temple, 40 kilometers from the city. The temple consisted of six square bases topped by three circular structures. It was constructed in the early part of the ninth century A.D. Even though it rained part of the day, this was a very interesting place to visit.

On the way back into the city we toured a silver factory. Watching the men and boys hand craft the silver into earrings, rings, plates, serving platters, and belt buckles was fascinating.

I visited the Sultan Palace to watch the rehearsal of the Yogya Classical Dance Group. The dress rehearsals are on Sunday from 10:30 in the morning to 12:30 in the afternoon. The only seating is on a floor mat. In a short while my backside became very uncomfortable so I stood at the edge of the crowd to watch this extravagant performance.

As I watched the dance, a young Indonesian boy asked where I lived. I told him I was from America, but remained aloof. I wasn't in the mood for another vendor or for another young man trying to pick me up. After awhile, though, I realized he only wanted to chat. He told me his name was Anok and that he was studying accounting at the local university. He shared some insight about the performance. When the rehearsal was finished, he asked the dancers if I could take a photograph of them and then he took one of me with them.

Anok explained the history to me as we wandered through the Sultan Palace. He asked if I had seen the Water Gardens. I had not, but they were on my list of sites to visit.

On our way to the Water Gardens we walked through Cemetri Island. These are ruins left after the war between Java and the Dutch. The ruins were once surrounded by water, but now there is only dust where the water once stood.

Finally, we arrived at the Water Gardens, formerly the residence and swimming pools of the king. Again, no water, only more dust and ruins.

Anok took me to visit his cousin who hand-made batiks. These small paintings on silk were mounted on cards. They were originals, so I purchased some for gifts.

Walking back, we again passed the palace area. Anok pointed out a wedding party. As we approached the gala affair, Anok asked the bride and groom if I could take a photograph of them having their first meal together as husband and wife. They agreed and smiled for me. Their wedding attire was very different from ours in the U.S., with no white.

As the day ended, Anok and I exchanged addresses. Having him for my special tour guide for the day was a pleasure. Not all the Indonesians are like Anok. Many of them are only interested in talking to you if they have something to gain, or something to sell. Others want to be friendly because you are a westerner, which to them means rich. Well, according to their standards, I guess we are.

At times it was annoying to walk down the street and have people constantly say, "What's your name, Madam?" "Where are you going?" "Where are you from?" These questions were repeated, it seemed, a hundred times a day. At times I wanted to scream "It's none of your business!" But of course, I didn't. Peace of mind came when I just accepted the questions and walked on.

I flew from Yogya to Jakarta. Previous I planned to take a train, but after learning it would be an all-night train I chose to fly. I remembered only too vividly how tired I was when I arrived from Bali after traveling all night on a train.

The plane arrived in Jakarta in the late afternoon. I went to tourist information to find a room for one night.

My last night in Indonesia was luxurious. At least it seemed so compared to the other places I had stayed. For US$27 I had a king-size bed, a telephone, television, air conditioning, and hot water!

I sat in my luxurious room reviewing the past six weeks in Indonesia. Being at the mercy of so many lunatic drivers, I was amazed I was still alive and free of injury. It was a miracle there were so few accidents with all the people and animals on the roads. My guardian angels had watched over me and everyone and everything in my path.

I wonder what it is like in Indonesia today?

India
- The Ashram -

My plane landed in Bombay, India, a little after 11:00 at night. I spent 45 minutes retrieving my luggage and changing currency into Indian rupees. According to information I received earlier from the ashram, a car would be there. When I did not see a contact person holding a sign with "Ganespuri" written on it, I approached a western woman standing by the curb. I asked if she was going to the ashram.

She said no. She and her husband were from England, and were spending the night in a hotel nearby, waiting for a flight for Goa the next morning.

I walked back to the waiting room for one last look, hoping someone was there with transportation to the ashram in Ganespuri. Then the realization hit me. The note I sent from Java to the ashram, explaining I was coming a day earlier, had not been received. I walked back outside and approached the lady from England, explaining my situation. She said she felt confident I could get a room in their hotel and invited me to share the taxi. I gladly accepted.

The worry of how to get to the ashram the next day made for a restless night. The next morning I tried to phone the ashram and could not get through. I found out later that getting a phone call through in India might take a while.

I went down to the desk to ask for suggestions from the clerk. He suggested I hire a car and driver for the two-hour drive to the ashram. Following the clerk's advice, I asked for a recommendation. He called a local driver and made the necessary arrangements.

The roads, again, were crowded with people and animals. The motor scooters of Thailand and Bali were replaced by little three-wheeled cars, similar to golf carts.

I was thrilled to be in India. It was a dream come true. The elderly have deep character lines in their faces. I saw pure, innocent beauty in the faces of the children. I was extremely pleased to find that most people in India speak English. There are different dialects in each of their states so they learn English as a common language. Even most beggars on the street speak English.

The buildings along the road displayed the glory and the sorrow of India. Attractive buildings were followed by clusters of shacks. In some places, the families lived in tents. Trash was piled high. India's poverty was all around.

Once out of Bombay there was not much to see, so I sat back and relaxed.

After a while we passed a sign that read "Ashram" and a short distance later I saw a high fence topped with barbed wire. Lush green foliage and brightly colored flowers lined the fence.

We turned the corner and looming in the distance were the elegant, tall, white pillars framing the entrance to Gurudev Siddha Peeth, the ashram.... a wonderland compared to all the poverty evident along the road.

I asked the driver to wait while I checked my reservation. They had not received my note, but assigned me to a bed in the women's dormitory on the terrace. My bed would be available by 3:00 that afternoon. I paid the driver the equivalent of $35 in American currency and he drove away. I stored my backpack with the luggage of others who were waiting for their rooms to be ready.

A pleasant lady at the desk directed me to the restaurants. There were two—one a vegetarian restaurant and the other with authentic Indian food. The latter was included in the price of lodging. A small fee was charged for the vegetarian restaurant, which I chose. There was a large display of appetizing foods. I filled my tray and joined a lone diner who introduced himself as Gary from New York.

An attractive French lady with flaming red hair joined us. She had taken a Hindu name, "Neelabindo." The word translates into blue bird. Neelabindo and I related to each other immediately. After lunch she escorted me to my room on the terrace. She had been living at the ashram for over a year and planned to remain indefinitely.

At the designated time I went to the office to officially check in. I was informed that I would be changing rooms. I was pleased to learn that I was moving into a condo with five other ladies. This was good news. The women's dorm on the third floor had twenty beds! They told me they had upgraded my accommodations because my friend from the Siddha Yoga Center in Hong Kong had made my reservations. I thanked Dale and Pat Keller in Hong Kong for helping me to be upgraded. They now live in Seattle, Washington.

I was asked to pay in advance for the month. It came to $126, or $4.20 a day! And, if I chose to have Indian food for lunch and dinner, those two meals would be free. I usually ate one meal in the Indian restaurant and paid for breakfast and one other meal in the vegetarian restaurant.

Neelabindo and I walked into the small typical Indian village of Ganespuri, about a mile from the ashram. Small children with tattered clothing and dirty faces were the norm. At first this tore at my heart, but as I looked closer I saw joyous light in the large, black eyes. Their laughter came from their hearts. The Indian children were so beautiful to me.

Neelabindo and I visited the temple that is dedicated to Swami Muthananda, the man who founded the ashram of Siddha Peeth. He was the guru of the ashram until his death. He trained Gurumayi from a small girl to take his place as guru.

Before entering the temple we purchased flowers from an Indian girl to be placed at the altar. We knelt for a few moments of meditation before walking to the altar for a blessing. I let Neelabindo go first, following her every move.

The swami behind the altar put holy water in my right hand. I drank it as I saw my friend do. The he passed his hand over my face and placed a small red dot of ashes in the middle of my fore-head. I felt a surge of energy bolt through my body. As we exited the temple I was overcome with such emotion that tears came to my eyes. I thanked Neelabindo for taking me there. We hugged and as we embraced the entire area became alive with the music of birds. Looking up, I saw hundreds of birds singing in the tall trees above. Their songs were so loud it was almost deafening. Had the birds felt the same energy I felt? Later I was told that these birds sound off every day at a certain time. I think we just happened to be under the trees at a magical moment. I know it certainly enhanced the powerful, loving energy I felt.

Residents of the ashram, both men and women, dress in typi-cal Indian dress. Not the sari, which is more formal attire, but a two-piece outfit, a knee-length dress with long pants. The Indians call this a "punjabi". I walked into the village and purchased a white punjabi and bought lovely flowered material to have one made. I purchased a couple of colorful scarves popular with the women. They wore the scarves around their necks for a more feminine look.

My friend warned me of the chilly evenings, suggesting I pur-chase a wool shawl. The evenings and early mornings were quite chilly. The wool shawl was used often.

I went to Gurudev Siddha Peeth in Ganespuri not knowing what to expect, but assumed it would be a month of relaxing and meditating. I knew very little about Siddha Yoga or about Gurumayi, their lovely guru, or about India in general.

Well, let me tell you, was I in for a big surprise! Each day began at 4:00 in the morning with two or three laps around the ashram grounds. At 5:30, it was time for the Guru Gita, translated as "Song of the Guru", group singing and chanting for an an hour and a half. We sat on the floor on small pillows for this long period of time. It took a while for my legs, backside, and back to adjust to this position.

Breakfast was served at 7:00 followed by two periods of "seva" which is service work. One period was from 8:00 until 11:30 in the morning; the second from 2:30 until 5:30 in the afternoon. Afterwards, we practiced yoga for 45 minutes. I desperately needed the yoga class to limber up for the two long chanting sessions each day.

Each of us was assigned seva. My stint was in the bakery, which I thought rather humorous. I had literally given up cooking and baking when my youngest turned 15. Each person was given a job that was entirely different from their normal lifestyle.

I loved working in the bakery. When my daughters were young I baked a lot, but as they grew into teenagers we were all watching our waistlines so I stopped. Here was an opportunity to rekindle an enjoyable pastime.

We were a compatible group. No mater how menial the task, we pitched in to help each other. Monique, our capable French manager, was no exception. Our bakery team was an international group. The United States, Australia, New Zealand, France, Italy, and India were represented. We had fun, and got the job done! The food and the baked goods in the ashram were outstanding. I welcomed both the walking and the yoga to stay in shape.

After yoga class I barely had time to shower and change for dinner and then, at 8:15 in the evening, another hour of chanting.

These sessions were not mandatory, but I always went. Chanting was in Hindu with English translation. For me it was truly soothing and relaxing. I felt a spiritual energy surrounding us. We were gathered in love and I felt enlivened.

By 9:30 I was in bed, asleep. Up at 4:00 every morning and in bed by 9:30 every evening. So much for 30 days of relaxation!

I learned of the 1994 earthquake in California while standing in line at the ashram's bank. My heart stopped for a moment. My daughters and their families lived in Los Angeles! I left the line and ran to the office to use the international phone. When the lady heard my name, she said, "We just received a fax for you."

Thank goodness I had sent my daughter, Suzie, the phone and fax numbers of the ashram.

With my eyes blurry with tears, I read, "We are all fine. No one hurt and only a small amount of damage. All phone lines are down."

I quickly sent a return fax to let her know I had received hers. I would call when I could get through. I walked back to the bank saying a silent prayer of thanks.

Siddha Yoga has many followers who have practiced its teachings for years. Centers are located all over the world. There is an ashram in South Fallsburgh, New York, as well as the one I attended in India. Many of the followers have not been to India, nor have they met or seen Gurumayi. Here I was, brand new, experiencing Siddha Yoga for the first time, and Gurumayi arrived four days after I did! She was scheduled to be at the ashram for a few months. That meant that I would have the opportunity to be in her presence the entire time I was there. Even as a newcomer I knew this was a privilege and an honor.

Every morning Gurumayi sat in a large, ornately decorated chair as her followers came to kneel in front of her to honor her. This ceremony is called "darsha." Many gave her a gift of money or flowers. If a person had something significant to ask her, or if they were new, there was a special line in which to stand. As a new person, I was encouraged to join the special line to be introduced to Gurumayi.

I was in awe as I came face to face with this incredibly lovely Spiritual Being. She smiled when I was introduced, saying, "Where did you get your name?"

I was accustomed to people asking me where I got the name Quay, as it is unusual. But I was surprised when she asked me.

"From my mother," I blurted out. Then I was motioned on to allow the next person to be acknowledged. (I now use Marie as my first name, but part of that trip around the world I chose to be called Quay or Quay Marie.)

To the dedicated followers of Siddha Yoga, it is a great honor to have those moments each day in Gurumayi's presence. I felt uncomfortable kneeling to worship another human being so I only went twice a week.

At breakfast one morning I sat next to a swami, one of the Hindu religious teachers at the ashram. I told him my feelings. He suggested I think of Gurumayi as one who had ascended to her Higher Self and that I was worshipping that essence of her. Put that way I felt more comfortable with the ritual of darsha.

One of the many highlights of my stay in the ashram was participating in a Hindu wedding. One of my roommates, Myra, was being married and she asked me to be part of the pre-wedding ceremonies. I did not have a sari for the very special occasion, so Myra lent me one of hers.

Hindu religious tradition is for the bride to have her hands decorated the night before her wedding. An artist draws ornate designs on her hands and fingers. The ink is black in color when applied, but as it dries it turns orange. The designs were elegant. I was invited to watch this ceremony because I was a participant in the pre-marriage ceremony.

On the day of the wedding, we five ladies whom Myra had chosen to be part of pre-marriage ceremony arrived at her room at 4:30 in the morning. She had moved into a private room a few days before. I followed the cue of the others. We took turns smearing a yellow herb cream on her feet, legs, hands and face. Then a red and orange dot was placed in the middle of her forehead.

When finished we went to the room of the groom and did the same for him. I didn't ask, but thought this probably was a purifying of the bride and groom before the ceremony.

Myra looked stunning in her exquisite sari of different shades of orange, red, and gold. This young, tall woman with reddish-blond hair, who is naturally beautiful, was glowing this morning.

Carlo, the groom, was attired in an all-white punjabi with a white headdress. They both wore garlands of white flowers accented with red roses.

The ceremony lasted four hours as the mantras were chanted in Sanskrit. As the ceremony unfolded I could see, in my mind's eye, how the traditions of centuries past were being reenacted in this powerful Hindu wedding ceremony.

After the ceremony, a select few of us were invited to an Indian lunch with the bride and groom. That evening this same group was invited to join Myra and Carlo for an evening feast.

Carlo is originally from Italy so we were served Italian food. There were platters of salads, antipasto, risotto, and several types of pasta. It was more food that could ever be consumed by the 100 people in attendance, but we did our very best.

Being an intimate part of a Hindu wedding was a once-in-a-lifetime experience, one I will always remember. I will forever be grateful to Myra and Carlo for including me in their special day.

The thirty days in the ashram were an incredible experience. I left feeling very connected with my Higher Self, and eager to see and experience more of India and its people.

India
- The Country -

Before I left the United States, I wrote a young Tibetan monk I have been sponsoring for a number of years. I began sponsoring Jampa when the Dalai Lama visited San Diego. I had the honor of meeting the Dalai Lama and was invited to an evening of chanting and dancing performed by a group of monks traveling with him. That evening I was given the opportunity to sponsor a young monk living in their monastery in India. I pledged to help him financially for an indefinite period of time.

In the letter I asked Jampa for permission to visit him at the monastery. His reply was enthusiastic. He sent directions to the town of Hubli near the monastery, located in Mundgod in central India.

After leaving the ashram, I took a bus to Bombay, where I inquired about transportation to Hubli. My first choice was the train but I was informed that train travel had been canceled. The tracks were being reworked. I booked a reservation on a bus leaving at 6:00 the next evening. It would be a twelve-to thirteen-hour bus ride. I had not used public transportation yet in India, so I was not sure what to expect.

I paid my very inexpensive fare and said a prayer for safety, comfort, and tolerance.

I grabbed a taxi to the Egyptian Embassy to obtain a visa for Egypt, the next country on my itinerary. This had not been purchased earlier because a visa for Egypt is only valid if purchased two months before entry into the country.

The clerk at the embassy recommended I stay at the Kemp Corner Hotel, centrally located and close to shopping. It was a little pricey for India at that time, at US$17 per night.

I called Bangalore, India, to reach a Servas couple concerning accommodations with them after a visit with Jampa, the young monk in Hubli. The Servas hosts said they would be delighted; knowing I would have a place to stay as I ventured farther south in India, I felt relieved.

The next day I took a taxi to the bus that would go to Hubli. The bus was late leaving and seemed to take forever to make its way out of the city. Much to my surprise, I found the bus quite comfortable. My seat-mate was an elderly Indian woman who was so small and quiet I forgot she was beside me.

A big problem: no toilets. The driver didn't stop often for potty call. When he did stop, it was in an area where the only place for privacy was behind a bush. Luckily I had my toilet tissue with me! If you plan to travel out of the United States, keep this in mind.

We arrived in Hubli, not in twelve or thirteen hours, but sixteen hours later. I got off the bus and stood thinking, "Now what do I do?" A young man came over and asked if I was going to the monastery in Mundgod. I was taken by surprise and quickly answered, "Yes!" He said he and his friend were going there and they would be honored to show me the way. I walked across the street to the bus station with the two young men carrying my backpacks. From Mundgod we boarded a small shuttle bus which took us to the monastery. On both occasions I tried to pay for their bus tickets but they waved away my offer.

One of the boys spoke English rather well. He told me that his brother was a monk in the monastery. His parents live in the Tibetan Colony there.

We arrived at the monastery and they were still carrying my bags. The boys helped me find the building where Jampa, my little monk, lived. I gave each of them one of the mother-of-pearl keys, the gift I give to people as a gesture for world peace - a "key to peace." My heart was touched when the young man who spoke English removed a woven bracelet from his wrist, very similar to those I had been taught to make, and gave it to me.

They went on their way and I stood there not believing what had happened. It had all been so easy. It was truly a miracle that they had asked if I was going to the monastery.

The next thing I knew, I was standing in front of a young man with, short, black, straight hair and sparkling brown eyes. He was smiling and holding out his hand to me. This was Jampa Tserling. I still thought of him as "my little monk" because he was only eight years old when I became his sponsor. Now he was about fifteen and because he is Tibetan, he was small for his age. But his ready smile and calming nature made him seem like a giant.

The older monks took it upon themselves to show me around. In very broken English they explained to me a little about life in a monastery.

Many of the boys enter the monastery when they are three years old. When they are older, they choose whether to stay or leave. About 5,000 boys were enrolled in the monastery. I spent only that day and a good part of the next day there. My goal was to meet Jampa, to see his face and hear his voice. He was being excused from his normal schedule while I was there and I did not want to interfere with his studies any longer than necessary. With my goal accomplished, I was ready to depart.

A car and driver arrived for my trip back to Hubli. As a special treat, Jampa was allowed to leave the monastery, along with an older monk, to accompany me to the bus station. As we said good-bye, Jampa draped a long, white silk scarf, a symbol of protection, around my neck and gave me a special handbag with "Tibet" inscribed on it.

After meeting Jampa, I knew he had not been the one writing letters to me for all the years we corresponded. He does not speak any English. Seeing him in person had a tremendous impact, and now my sponsorship of this young Tibetan monk was even more profound. I sponsored Jampa until after he reached his eighteenth year.

I booked a seat on an all-night bus from Hubli to Bangalore, arriving at 7:00 the next morning. After waiting an hour, I called Sophie and Sumant, the Servas hosts in Bangalore, to find a convenient time for arriving at their home. Their greeting was warm and friendly, inviting me to come immediately.

I was treated like a queen by this kind, loving Indian couple. Sophie loved to cook. Discovering that I liked Indian food, she prepared the most delicious meals.

Sophie was a lovely, vivacious woman in her early fifties. She was a watercolor artist as well as the owner and director of a Montessori school where she teaches painting to the children. Sumant was an engineer with a large company just outside of Bangalore. He was on the quiet side with a kind gentleness about him that I was drawn to immediately. They would not be thought wealthy by our standards, but I am sure they are considered wealthy by the people of their country.

Sophie had two very young Indian sisters working for her. These girls were probably ten and twelve years old. They took their wages home to help their large family survive.

Bangalore is a lovely town even though it's a bit congested with traffic and pollution. I saw most of the city on my own, as well as being escorted by my hosts a few times in the evenings. Bangalore was somewhat of a stopping-off place for me. Having Sophie and Sumant's guidance for arrangements for other destinations was a tremendous help, saving me a lot of precious time.

I traveled south to Sai Baba's ashram in Puttaparthi. I shared the three-hour taxi ride with a man, also en route to the ashram. My experience in this ashram was very different from Gurumayi's in Ganespuri. Sai Baba's ashram is much larger and seemed to be geared to Indians rather than westerners. I shared a room with two other ladies, one from Sweden and one from Spain. The room was simple, with thick mats on the floor for sleeping.

Sai Baba holds darsha the first thing in the morning and the procedure is different. Here the men and women line up separately, then are escorted into the courtyard by rows.

Sai Baba was not sitting and waiting for his audience to come to him. He was nowhere to be seen. Each of us was provided with a pad for sitting. Seated as comfortably as possible, I noticed all heads turn, so I turned mine and saw Sai Baba enter. This procedure allows his followers the opportunity to give an offering or just be in his presence.

Sai Baba walked to his left, the opposite direction from where I sat. As he passed, those close enough reached out. Some bowed to him and gave him small gifts. Others tried to touch his feet. The Guru's feet are believed to be extremely holy. It is believed by many that Sai Baba is our modern day "Jesus" because he has been known to heal the sick. Who knows? Perhaps he is.

I said good-bye to my roommates the next morning and took a shared taxi back to the train station in Bangalore to take the train to Mysore in southern India.

Traveling in India proved to be rather enjoyable. I had been warned before arriving that it was difficult, but that was not true for me. The buses from Bombay and the train ride to Mysore, even though crowded, were certainly comfortable and safe. I felt at ease amongst the Indian people. I found them friendly and helpful, except for the beggars, most of whom were aggressive.

From Mysore I took a few day trips with organized tours. The city tour was a delightful excursion, which took us not only to the sites in the city but also out into the country. Driving through the countryside, I saw numerous rice paddies; I had not expected to see this in India.

In Mysore, cows were roaming the streets. The poor cows were starving to death. Several times I saw cows eating paper or plastic bags from garbage cans, hoping to discover a morsel of food. So much poverty in India—too many people and they just keep bearing children.

Before going to Mysore, I arranged with Sophie and Sumant to stay with them when I returned. Back in Bangalore, I made airplane reservations for a flight to Goa and then on to Bombay with a flight to Katmandu, Nepal. With my travel arrangements made for the next couple of weeks, I walked to the post office to mail a package home. My backpack was again filled to the brim with treasures from India. Mailing parcels by surface mail was relatively inexpensive. The large package I sent cost approximately US$25.

I said good-bye to Sophie. Sumant drove me to the airport. It was with heavy heart that I left this caring and loving couple. We exchanged addresses. We corresponded for a couple of years, but I have now lost contact with them.

I called home after settling in my hotel in Goa, India, only a block from the sea. Talking to my oldest daughter, Kathy, was rewarding. She had exciting news for me. My young granddaughter, now almost a year old, had just started walking. I cried when she told me. I was missing so much of the growth of my first grandchild, but grandma had this urge to travel, to see the world, and that was just what she was doing.

After the phone call, walking over to the beach helped ease the sadness. This was not the beauty of the beaches of Thailand or Indonesia, but being near the water once again felt comforting.

The beach was filled with Indians and westerners. The Indian men wore bathing suits but the Indian women go into the water in a punjabi. That doesn't seem quite fair to me. I guess equal rights for men and women had not arrived in India. Have they now? I doubt it.

After a closer look, I found my hotel to be inadequate. It was not the cleanest and the bed was as hard as a rock. I checked out and moved into the Tourist Resort right on the beach. I obtained a clean room, a comfortable bed, and a balcony with a view of the water for the equivalent of US$6.90.

I ate dinner in the resort restaurant. The food was delicious. I enjoyed a vegetarian dish that tasted very much like a meal Sophie had cooked. It came with naan, the typical Indian bread, very similar to our pita bread.

The next morning I walked along the water to the flea market in Ajnuna, a small village nearby. I came upon a small river en route. I wasn't sure if I was going in or not. A man approached and I asked him if the river was safe to cross. He assured me it was. When he learned I was going to the flea market, he said, "Why not come along with me?"

The walk around the point was beautiful, though at times it was difficult. The path was hilly and there were boulders over which we had to climb. I forgot to bring water and was very thirsty when we arrived. I thanked the man and after we said good-bye, I rushed off to purchase a bottle of water.

If you go to Goa, the flea market in Anjuna is a must-see. Not only were there some incredible buys, but visually it was fantastic. Some of the women vendors were decorated colorfully, wearing many bangles on their wrists and forearms. It is quite common to see Indian women with studs in their noses.

One woman vendor was decorated more lively than the others. I chatted with her for a while and then asked if I could take a photograph. When she agreed, I took the photograph, thanked her and started on my way. She came after me very aggressively, wanting to know why I did not buy something from her. I explained that she did not have anything that I needed or wanted to purchase. She did not like my answer and I could hear her yelling loudly behind me as I walked on. That was not a pleasant experience.

I wandered through the market, but after the ordeal with the bangle lady, I wasn't in a shopping mood any longer.

Most of my experiences with the Indian people were pleasant. I gave in to some of the beggars but was selective. There is so much poverty in the country that it is not any wonder that the people are sometimes angry and aggressive toward westerners.

After a few more days relaxing on Calangut Beach, swimming in the warm water, taking photographs and enjoying the people, I bought a ticket to Panaji. My venture by bus, then ferry, to the town of Panaji went as smooth as silk. My loving God and all my guides were certainly with me.

Departing the ferry in Panaji I found a clean, inexpensive room near the Indian Airline ticket office. It would be an easy walk there the next morning to catch a bus to the airport for my flight to New Delhi. I would have a one-night layover before my flight to Nepal. In New Delhi I booked at the youth hostel in Chanahyapuri, near the airport.

My evening in Panaji was delightful. I ventured down to the Mondovi River and went on a sunset boat cruise. We cruised down the river for two hours while the Goan folk dancers entertained us. It was a surprisingly enjoyable evening for a very low price, equivalent to US$1.62.

I kept a journal during my travels. Not only was it healing therapy, but a great way to log all my experiences and the names of the different towns and areas. As I sat down to write that evening I looked at the date I had just written and panicked. Had I missed my flight to New Delhi? I took out my calendar and found I had written the last few dates down wrong! I was on schedule and had not missed my flight. When one is traveling for an extended period of time it is easy to get days mixed up. It is imperative to ask someone the day and the date often, to avoid missing a plane or some other mode of transportation.

Katmandu, Nepal

The flight from Panaji to New Delhi was delayed for four hours. Once I arrived in New Delhi, I had a pleasant night's stay in the youth hostel.

I was excited the next morning as I boarded the airplane to Nepal. Before long we were airborne. Seemingly moments later, as I looked out the window of the big jet, I saw snow-capped mountains. I thought, "This must be the Himalayas." Like an answer to my thoughts, the captain's voice rang out loud and clear on the intercom. "We are now flying over the Himalayas." I was experiencing another dream, in full color!

I learned from reading my guide book that a visa is required in Nepal, and could be purchased at the airport. While I waited in line for my visa, an American told me that as a United States citizen I would have to pay the $40 in U.S. currency.

Fred, the man in line with me, was from San Francisco. He had been to Katmandu a couple of months before. I asked him about places to stay. He suggested we share a taxi into town where he knew of a place we could stay. We checked into Hotel Potola. My room was 100NR (Nepal rupees), which was equivalent to two American dollars! Now for this price I did not have a private bath and shower, but for me that luxury was not necessary. The toilet and showers were located only a few feet down the hall. The hotel was located in the Thamel area. This, I learned, was the best place for good restaurants and great shopping. (It may not be today so it would need to be checked out.)

Fred and I went to dinner. I told him I was a vegetarian and he knew exactly where to go. I chose eggplant lasagna served with rice. Fred told me the rice in Nepal sometimes has little stones in it so we asked for garlic bread as a replacement. The meal was excellent, and the company as well. Fred was, I guess, about forty then, tall, maybe 6'4". He was new to the teachings of Buddhism. His return to Katmandu was to reenter the monastery. This stay would be for meditation and the practice of silence.

After the delectable meal and pleasant conversation, we paid our bill, walked back to the hotel, and said goodnight. Fred left for the monastery the next day.

I went to the hotel travel agency to inquire about things to do in and around Katmandu. I knew I wanted to go to Pokhara to hike and to get a closer look at the Himalayas. The travel agent told me about a white-water rafting trip down the Trisuli River, the most popular in Nepal. White-water rafting! I had always wanted to go rafting, but here in Nepal I heard myself argue. This I said quietly to myself, *Feel the Fear and Do It Anyway!*

While the travel agent explained the details of the trip, a feeling of excited anticipation replaced the feelings of doubt. It was to be a three-day, two-night trip, camping out along the river. The price was $65 for transportation to the river, the rafting, tents, sleeping bags, and meals. I signed up then and there!

The hotel clerk said I could leave my large backpack and any valuables, such as traveler checks and credit cards, stored in the safe. This was common practice for many hotels. In most cases your belongings were safe. It is important, however, to make sure your bags are locked and that small valuables be placed in plastic bags sealed with tape, so they cannot be opened easily.

The first day, I took a four-hour bus ride to the river. As far as I know, I was the only one on that particular bus going rafting. I found fear and doubt returning. I kept telling myself to relax, to trust, and all would be just fine.

After the others arrived, we walked down to the river shore where helmets and life vests were issued. There were two rubber rafts with seven people per raft and two guides. I was assigned to a raft with six men. One fellow was from the United States, two from Denmark, two from France, and one from Japan.

We rafted for three-and-a-half hours, including a half-hour break for lunch. Some of the areas were rather treacherous but mostly it was just a pleasant cruise down the river. I was happy the water was not white the entire day. Trying to balance myself while fighting the rapids drained a lot of energy. Once I was knocked off my seat but luckily landed on the bottom of the raft and not in the water!

We all had oars and had to pitch in to keep the raft moving, especially in the rougher water. I became so involved with using my oars and following instructions from the guides, I forgot to be scared.

It was an exciting day. Even though the guides were young, they were strong and well-trained in river rafting. They seemed to know every inch of the river and what to expect next. I felt completely safe.

When we reached our final destination that day I found that most of the others were with us only for the one day. This left the two young men from Denmark, Mike and Ras, me, and the two guides.

A van followed the raft along the river, carrying food and tents. When we docked, the drivers of the van and our guides set up the tents and prepared dinner while the three of us sat by the river, quietly talking over the experiences of the day.

We were served tea, but I did not drink it. It was my rule to not drink tea or coffee while in India or Nepal unless I knew for a fact that the water had been boiled.

The guides brought us soup, french fries, and chipati (unleavened Indian bread). We ate heartily, thinking that was our meal. Then they brought our dinner of rice, noodles, cauliflower, and other fresh vegetables.

After dinner, the young men built a fire and set up our tents and sleeping bags before cleaning up from the meal. When finished, they joined us around the open fire. I became very fond of the four young men taking care of us. Two of them were fourteen years of age, one was nineteen, and one twenty-two. They spoke adequate English and were pleasant company.

Nepal was much chillier than India. I was glad I had come prepared with some sweats. I went to bed about 8:00 each evening, not because I was that tired but because it was that cold.

The next morning three other people joined us, a young man from Japan and an Indian couple. The woman wore her punjabi aboard the raft, and she had a sprained ankle! She sat in the middle of the raft without an oar. I was astonished. I was having a hard time staying in the raft with an oar in each hand, wearing shorts, and with both legs in fine working order!

This was a full day on the river. Time dragged as we encountered fewer rapids to negotiate. With less activity and wet clothing we became a little chilly at times. We stopped for lunch around 2:00 that afternoon. The guides spread out a nice selection of potato salad, canned baked beans, canned tuna, and some tasty brown bread with peanut butter and jelly.

After a few more hours, through several challenging rapids, we made camp for the night. Another enormous meal and early to bed.

A couple of hours on the river the next day and our adventure was over. It had been an exciting experience for me. I had stretched my capabilities one more time, doing something I always wanted to do, not letting fear hold me back.

After eating lunch at the river's edge, I said good-bye to Ras, Mike, and the guides. Another adventure awaited me, so I was off to the bus stop for a ride to Pokhara.

When the bus arrived it was packed. The only place to sit was on a step near the door. It was hard and uncomfortable and the roads were bumpy. Soon a few people got off and I was able to stand in the aisle. This was better. I could view the scenery. Looking down the mountainside, I could see the river upon which I had just been rafting.

I arrived in Pokhara at 8:00 that evening after a long, hard five-hour bus ride. The "hawkers" were there to induce as many as they could to "their" hotel. I was so tired I just said "yes" to the first man who approached me. The hotel was close by and being neat and clean was a plus.

After settling in, I looked at my guide book and discovered this hotel to be in the exact area I planned to stay. The proprietor brought a towel and a comforter for the bed. Now, at a higher altitude, the nights would be cooler.

Pokhara, located on the edge of a lake, is a rugged and enchanting mountainous area. I was eager to take a short hike into the mountains. My guide book told me of a place called Saranghot. I was at 5,222 feet of elevation, with a fabulous view. The best place to start the walk is at Binde Basini Temple. After a few wrong turns and stops to ask directions, I found the temple. Once there, I spoke with two young men who lived in the area. I asked them about the trail head and they agreed to show me where it began.

As we walked, one of the young men said he would go along with me as a "friend" and did not expect any money. I thought about it for a moment and decided to trust him. His name was Narayan, a pleasant, small-boned young man of maybe twenty-two or twenty-three.

The day was hot, the pathways dusty, rocky, and at times steep. We stopped often for a breather and a drink of water. Even though the sun was bright, the view was hazy.

Just short of the top, we realized there would not be a view of the Annapurna Mountains on this day. At first I was disappointed. The reason I had come to Pokhara was to see the beautiful snow-capped mountains of Annapurna. The disappointment faded as I let my imagination take over. In my mind's eye I could visualize how lovely this view would be on a clear day.

We descended on the lake side. Then I knew why the guide book had suggested beginning the walk near the temple. Most of the way I was walking down very steep stairs. I was really feeling the descent in my knees so I could imagine how tough it would have been walking up those stairs.

The entire trek took eight hours! That included the two hours I spent trying to find the temple.

When we returned to the lake-front, I treated Narayan to lunch. He ordered pizza, I chose lasagna. After eating, we exchanged addresses. I gave him a few dollars for his expert guidance before we parted.

I would like to return to this intriguing area at another time to stay longer, and to be in top physical condition, so that trekking in this rough, rugged area of Nepal would be more enjoyable.

I took a minibus back to Katmandu. It was an eight-hour trip that should have taken much less time, but the driver stopped often. On the bus I sat beside a young man from Seattle, Washington. In Katmandu, the bus let us off in an area with which I was not familiar, but my seat companion knew his way around. Together we walked to the vicinity of my hotel. The city atmosphere seemed extremely noisy and polluted compared to the river and mountain from which I had just come.

I checked back into the Portola Hotel, a different room but basically the same. Shopping and eating was not a problem in Katmandu, as there were many excellent restaurants with menus to fit any appetite. Shopping values were excellent, as prices were dirt cheap in the '90s. There were so many shops from which to choose, I sometimes became confused. As in most places, bartering was common.

The people of Nepal were similar to the people in India and yet there was a difference. I was touched by the beauty of the children as I had been in India. But Nepal was not as crowded, nor did I see as many beggars.

New Delhi, India

My flight from Katmandu to New Delhi was late but that happened often on Indian Airlines. From the New Delhi airport, I caught a bus into town. I sat next to an American lady. She had hotel reservations and invited me to share the double room with her. I agreed. I would be in town only for the night as I was taking the train to Agra the next morning.

The Jukaso Inn was air-conditioned which was a blessing. It was really hot, especially after being in the coolness of Nepal for a few days. I paid my share, $16. That was a lot of money compared to my normal rate of two to four American dollars. It was a much nicer hotel and I felt secure in leaving my large bag, which contained a number of rolls of exposed film.

I took an auto-rickshaw to the New Delhi train station. (An auto-rickshaw was propelled by a motor, not a person. Has it changed? I have no idea. I planned to take the Taj Express to Agra. I asked a person behind the counter where to buy a ticket. He sent me on a wild goose chase and by the time I found the right window, they were sold out. The only tickets left were second-class on the regular train. With ticket in hand, I made my way to platform No. 3 from which the train to Agra departed.

I bought an orange for breakfast. While I was eating the orange and reading my guide book on India, a young lady interrupted, asking if I was going to Agra. I told here I was and we started a conversation. She was from Cairo, Egypt. When I told her Cairo was my next destination, she said she would like to give me her phone number. About that time the train arrived and everyone made a mad dash to board. She yelled out, "I'll find you in Agra."

An Indian man helped me squeeze aboard the overly-crowded train. In the mass of faces, I lost sight of the young woman with whom I had been talking. It looked as though there were no seats, but the Indian man ushered me into the middle of a group of locals. In fact, all I could see on the train were Indian people. I sat in the middle of four locals. There were five Indian people seated directly across from us.

The over-crowded train was hot and stuffy. Not only were all the seats taken, but people were standing and sitting in the aisles. The train was a half-hour late leaving the station. The seat was already uncomfortable. It was made of wooden planks, no padding! After we departed, I discovered the train ride would be four hours instead of two on the Taj Express. I also learned that the Taj Express departs from the *old* New Delhi station.

Even though the train ride was long, hot, and uncomfortable, being among so many locals was pleasurable. The other passengers were prepared for a four-hour trip. They brought snacks. I left the hotel thinking I would be on the Taj Express for only two hours.

So much for "thinking". The people were very kind, offering to share their food with me, but I declined their generous offers.

When we arrived in Agra, the Indian man helped me off the train and was sticking around. It was obvious he was planning to be my escort or who knows what. I politely told him I was meeting friends at first-class, thanked him, and walked away.

Just as I said that, I ran into Safaa, the Egyptian lady I met in New Delhi. We decided to take a tour of Agra together. Our first stop was the tourist office. All the tour buses had left for the day so the lady suggested we hire a taxi or a rickshaw to take us to Agra Fort, Little Taj, and The Taj Mahal.

The fort was just a fort but the other areas the taxi driver showed us were exquisite. Then we arrived at the Taj Mahal. It was more spectacular than I had expected. I took photograph after photograph. I wanted to capture every possible angle of this magnificent structure. We walked around, peeking in every little door, room, or passageway we could find. At an opening in a wall, we looked out and saw Little Taj in the distance. More photographs!

By 4:00 that afternoon we were hot, tired, and hungry. I ate the orange in the early morning and nothing but water since then. Safaa had not eaten either. The taxi driver suggested a restaurant nearby. We walked the short distance to "The Only Restaurant" (that was its real name), sat down, and were given menus.

It had been an extremely pleasant day. Safaa and I had blended famously. She is a lovely woman, and at that time she was very young with long, thick, black, wavy hair. Safaa was employed as a travel agent in Cairo where she had lived all her life.

During lunch I made the decision not to spend the night in Agra, or to go on to Jaipur as I originally planned. I was hot, tired, and needed to rest for a few days before flying to Cairo. I decided to return to New Delhi by train, that evening, with Safaa. She had a hotel room booked with two beds and invited me to share it. I gladly accepted.

Safaa was thrilled that I was coming to Cairo. Even though I had friends just outside of Cairo with whom I would be staying, she wanted me to come into the city and bunk at her apartment for a few days.

At the train station, first-class tickets for the Taj Express were sold out, so we bought second-class tickets. When the train arrived, Safaa suggested we take seats in the first-class section. There were plenty of empty seats in the first-class car. We chose two and sat down. When the conductor came to collect tickets, we paid a few extra rupees for our seats and enjoyed a comfortable ride back to Delhi. The next day I placed a call to Shaker in Cairo.

I met Shaker Kaleda in 1970 in San Diego, while he was visiting his brother Asaad, a close friend of mine. While I was planning my around-the-world trip I told Asaad I would be going to Egypt and he suggested I get in touch with his brother.

I called Shaker from my home in Idaho. He was pleased I was coming to Cairo and said I was welcome to stay in his home. He worked for Egypt Airlines at that time, and he was away often, therefore it was important I call him in plenty of time before my scheduled arrival. I dropped post cards along the way so he had a general idea when I might be in Cairo, but not a specific date.

Now I was placing the call to give him the date and time of arrival, as well as the airline and flight number.

When I reached him, he said he would be out of town the day I arrived but he would make arrangements with a friend to meet my plane. His sister, Isis, would also be there to take me to his apartment and entertain me until he arrived the next day.

After making arrangements for Cairo, I turned my attention to seeing New Delhi. Safaa would be leaving a couple of days before I did, so we went our separate ways. She wanted to shop and I wanted to see the sights of the city.

At the tourist office I booked an all-day tour for the next day to see New Delhi. I walked to the Jurasso Inn and picked up the luggage I had stored there for the trip to Agra, then caught a taxi back to the hotel.

Safaa returned about 7:00 that evening, her arms loaded with packages. She had indeed been on a shopping spree. She was leaving for Cairo the next day so we dressed up, each wearing one of the new dresses she had purchased. We went to the hotel dining room for dinner.

I was glad Safaa and I had met. She was a delightful person with whom to spend my last few days in India. I was eagerly looking forward to seeing her again in Cairo. It would be fun to have Shaker as well as a female friend with whom to do things.

The next day was long but enjoyable. The tour of New Delhi began at 8:30 in the morning. We didn't get off the bus much; the sights were pointed out to us.

One break from the bus ride was a tour of a carpet factory. Most things may be inexpensive in India, but their exquisite carpets were not. A small one caught my eye. I thought perhaps I would buy it and mail it home. I looked at the tag and it was US$1800! A large one was priced at $15,000! Those prices did not fit into my budget.

I needed to mail a package home again. I purchased many items while in Goa, Nepal, and New Delhi. I also had about 20 rolls of exposed film that I wanted to airmail. Opening the small bag I left at the Jurasso Inn, I discovered five rolls of the exposed film were missing!

At the beginning of my trip I began numbering each cartridge of film and kept a written log of each photograph. This was important. I knew I would be taking a lot of photographs and I would be gone a long time. I would never be able to remember the subjects or areas of each of these photos. That was why I numbered them. Knowing exactly what numbers were on the missing film containers, I went back to the hotel to complain. I knew I would never see my film again, but I at least wanted them to know I had been ripped off. I was sure that the thief saw film and didn't even consider that it might already be exposed. I had not locked that bag, another lesson I learned. And, like most lessons, it took a loss to learn it. We are so blessed today to have digital cameras or iPhones with which to take photos. Not only are they safer, but they weigh less and you don't have the shipping and film costs.

Two months in India had been a gratifying experience. I met so many nice people, saw so many intriguing places, and experienced so many new adventures. As I packed my bag, I realized how I eager I was to continue on to Egypt.

Egypt

Departing India, I switched from Singapore Airlines to Swiss Air. I landed in Zurich, Switzerland, for a four-hour layover before departing to Cairo.

Just being in the airport in Zurich was a culture shock—so modern and so clean! After months of being in third-world countries with poverty and dirt, Switzerland looked absolutely sterile to me.

While I waited for my flight I picked up my trusty *Lonely Planet* guide book on Egypt. As usual, it gave me information on everything from what to do, see, and eat to any travel restrictions.

I learned that once entering Cairo, I needed to register with the police before seven days passed, and that I would need a double entry visa because I wanted to go to Israel and return to Egypt. This double entry visa was obtained at the airport.

Before going through the security check in Zurich, I removed the film from my small bag to be hand-checked. Some of the X-ray machines caused distortion of the film back in those days. In the last six months I had been traveling, this had not been a problem with the security guards. However, this time when I asked the security to hand inspect my film, he refused. He told me the film would not be harmed. Not trusting this man's judgment, I asked for the manager. The manager arrived and still my request was refused. Realizing I had lost the argument, I placed my film on the conveyor belt and went through security check.

I guess they knew what they were talking about. I did not have any distorted photographs. Switzerland's security check may have been an exception because I continued to hand-carry my film through security check and was not stopped again.

The Swiss Alps were a sight to behold. I was glad that I would be returning in a few months to take a closer look.

I went through passport control at Cairo airport and found only a stamp was required for a re-entry visa.

Michele, Shaker's friend and the manager of Swiss Air and Cairo Airport, was there to meet me. After claiming my luggage, she guided me to the area where Shaker's sister, Isis, waited.

Isis was a short woman of about sixty-five. Her hair, once dark, was graying. Her lovely brown eyes sparkled when she said "hello". We liked each other immediately. During the taxi ride to Shaker's apartment, Isis told me a little about herself. She was a widow living in Alexandria. She came to Cairo often, not only to see her brother, but also to work as a part-time guide in the Cairo Museum.

Shaker's apartment is quite large; his parents lived there for many years before they passed away. Shaker, never having been married, at that time lived in the family home alone.

The apartment includes a large sitting room, a formal dining room, a kitchen with a small table for eating, three bedrooms, and one bath with a tub, shower, and bidet. The apartment was furnished with family antiques.

I had a bedroom with a full-size bed. Isis slept in another room furnished with twin beds. The master bedroom was reserved for Shaker. In the apartment there were family photographs everywhere. As I examined the photos of Shaker I began to remember him. Not having seen him in twenty-plus years, I knew he would have changed somewhat.

I was introduced to Shaker's housekeeper-cook, Fula. She was a tall, large-boned Egyptian woman. She did not speak English, but was always smiling and eager to help.

Shaker called from Montreal that evening. He would return the next day and was calling to make sure I had made it to his apartment. I felt very loved and well-cared for with these sensitive, considerate people.

Having a contact person for mail was convenient. Letters were waiting for me at Shaker's, as well as a package from home with warmer clothes. Cairo was chilly at that time of year and I especially needed these garments for the European segment of my trip coming up after Egypt.

Cairo is somewhat metropolitan so the clothes mailed to me would be fine for the cooler weather while hiking in Europe but not for the city. The first item on my agenda was to go shopping for new outfits to wear there. I found the styles of clothing in Cairo to be a little drab by California standards, but I bought two garments that would work.

My first day of sightseeing was spent at the Cairo Museum. Isis went with me. I felt blessed to have my very own private professional tour guide. The Cairo Museum is huge. It would have taken days to see the entire collection, so Isis guided me only to King Tut's Tomb and the exhibit of his personal possessions. Seeing all these fabulous antiques, so ancient yet still intact, was amazing.

Shaker returned later that day. We had both changed a lot. I thought he was more handsome in his maturity, and still had the captivating smile and sparkling brown eyes that I remembered from years past.

That evening, Shaker, the perfect host, took Isis and me to dinner in the Sonesta Hotel, which is known for its excellent restaurant. During dinner I mentioned to Shaker and Isis that I would love to see an Egyptian wedding. Well, guess what? A wedding reception was taking place in the hotel! I didn't see the ceremony, of course, but the reception was enough to be thoroughly impressed by.

The next day I took a taxi into Cairo to spend a few days with Safaa, the young lady I met in India. Her apartment was in the Zamalek district, a location with embassies, modern apartment buildings, and large sports clubs.

Safaa, a travel agent, booked an all-day trip to the pyramids for me. She also took care of my flight to Abu Simbel where I would join a group for a cruise down the Nile. I can't tell you how nice and convenient it is to have local friends when visiting a foreign country.

With Safaa's help it seemed like in no time I was on a bus to the outskirts of Cairo. There in the distance I could see the pyramids. For my entire life I have heard, read, and dreamed about the pyramids in Egypt. Finally I was only steps away!

As far as the eye could see was the great Sahara Desert and, as I turned in the other direction, I could see Cairo. What a contrast— the golden sand meeting the greenness of civilization. Standing there brought on a tremendous feeling of excitement for me.

Camels were everywhere, their owners beckoning tourists to take a ride or to have photographs taken with the animals. I had always visualized the Sahara Desert with camels. Now the picture was complete.

That evening I went with Safaa and a friend of hers to Cairo's famous bazaar, Khan el Khalili. It is huge. I was fascinated by all the goods. I, of course, spent my fair share on small gifts. Some of my favorite purchases were paintings done on papyrus.

As we wandered around the bazaar, I noticed a lot of people in cafes smoking from large water pipes, a common sight in Cairo. It is a custom, similar to our cigar smoking, considered classier than cigarette smoking. My granddaughter tells me that it is the rage in college today but they are called "hookah" in the States.

Lost one morning, trying to find the Cairo Tower, I asked directions from a nicely-dressed young man. He said to follow him and he would show me the way. I followed him, only to find myself in his father's perfume bottle shop. That day I learned to be leery of people who offer help in large cities. Many times they only want to sell something or want a "tip" for giving information.

Cairo is the center of Egypt. Estimates (back in 1994) of this city's population ranged from eleven to fifteen million - roughly one-quarter of Egypt's total. Attracting people from all over the country overwhelmed the city, causing it to be overcrowded. The massive increase in population resulted in overcrowded buses and snarled traffic jams. Everything seemed discolored; buildings, buses, and footpaths are brown or gray from smog and desert dust.

I found the Egyptian people remarkably friendly. In some of the museums I visited, the teenagers asked if they could have their photographs taken with me. I felt like a celebrity. I was flattered by the attentions of the Egyptian men as well, but I had to let them know when it was not appropriate to overstep my boundaries.

I went with Safaa and Paul, an American friend of ours, to the camel market. When in Cairo, this is a must-see! The Arabs bring their camels to the market to sell. I was fascinated to be surrounded by so many camels of all different sizes, colors, and personalities. One of my favorite scenes was of a small, black baby camel being fed with a bottle by his owner.

After the camel market, Safaa, Paul, and I hired a car to Saggari, an area in the desert. In Saggari I rode on a camel. When Paul took his ride, the owner of the camel dressed him in a red cloak and a large headdress, like a king. What a fun-filled experience that was. Two Americans, in the desert in Egypt, riding a camel. We were both thankful for Safaa, our special Egyptian tour guide.

That evening the three of us went to El Fishya, a tea house recommended by my guide book. The tea house was filled with mostly Egyptians. Having Safaa along to fill us in on the customs of her people was a plus. Many of the people were sharing water pipes. The Egyptians call them "sheesha". Paul ordered a sheesha for the three of us.

We passed it around the table, each taking a turn. I am a non-smoker but could not resist a couple of puffs just for the experience.

A few mornings later a taxi arrived at Safaa's to drive me to the airport for a flight to Abu Sibel in southern Egypt. There I would meet a tour group for a Nile cruise. As I settled myself aboard Egyptian Air, the flight attendant came to me and said, "The pilot would like to see you." Puzzled, I walked to the cockpit.

The pilot welcomed me aboard and then asked if there was anything he could do for me. I said, "Just get me there safely." He smiled and said, "Would you like to sit in the cockpit during takeoff?" My answer was a big grin. The flight attendant pulled out a jump seat, I sat down, and she strapped me in. As we taxied down the runway I said to the pilot, "You are obviously a friend of Shaker's." He replied with a nod and a smile.

I thought of Shaker and how thoughtful it was of him to arrange this for me. But quickly my attention was focused straight ahead as the big jet began to lift its nose. A short time later we were airborne. I returned to my seat with an invitation to return to the cockpit for the landing!

The takeoff was exciting, but it was nothing compared to the landing which felt as though we were speeding at 500 mph down towards the runway. The plane seemed to pick up speed as we touched the runway. What a thrill! Riding in the cockpit of a jet is something I would not be allowed to do in the United States. I will be eternally grateful to Shaker for those glorious moments.

We landed in Abu Simbel, where buses were waiting to take us to the temples. First to catch my eye were the four statues of Ramses II, symbolizing his different sides, and two statues representing his favorite wife, Queen Nefertari.

Inside the temples were carvings and old paintings that were unique. They used the residue or shavings from the carvings for paint and added color to the paint with flowers and plants.

Egypt was everything I had dreamed it to be and more. So ancient, so beautiful, and yet so modern. I loved the people, and the men loved me! Being a blond westerner in that part of the world can definitely build up the ego of any woman.

I was the only one from that group to travel on the Aswan. The others in Abu Simbel took a different tour. I was met in Aswan by an Arab man and was escorted to the ship for the Nile cruise.

Aboard the "Nile Bride" I checked in and was shown to room No. 218. This would be my home for the next five nights and four days. The cruise and the flight cost less than $500, with a little extra for refreshments aboard the ship.

The cabin was furnished with twin beds covered in bright-colored plaid spreads and matching drapes on the porthole. There was a love seat, a round table, and a small, attractive desk. I was more than pleased with these comfortable accommodations.

The steward informed me that lunch would be served soon. I hurriedly freshened up before heading for the dining room.

I sat with a couple from Denmark. They were taking an afternoon tour and invited me to join them, but when I arrived at the front desk I found that a different tour had been planned for me. I was to go to the mausoleum of Agha Khan and to the Botanical Gardens. I thanked the couple and waited for my guide. When he arrived I found it was just him and me for the afternoon.

A short distance from the ship we boarded a felucca, a small sailboat. I had seen these boats from a distance and hoped I'd get a chance to sail on one. Now here I was cruising on the Nile with my guide, Zachria, the captain of the small boat, and his twelve-year-old son.

In a short while we docked and walked up the steps of the mausoleum. From the top of the hill I was treated to a breathtaking view of the Nile, little white faluccas with their sails flapping in the breeze, and the town of Aswan.

The mausoleum is built of sandstone and granite, although the tomb was constructed of Italian marble. Agha Khan's wife had the tomb built in his honor along with space beside him that was reserved for her. A fresh red rose was placed on the tomb each day while a passage from a special book was read. How romantic! I felt tingly just being in such a loving space.

I ate an enjoyable dinner aboard the Nile Bride that evening of fresh fish, rice, fresh vegetables, and carrot salad. I went to bed early.

At 6:30 the next morning I awakened and realized the cruise was underway. I dressed quickly and walked up to the sun deck. The sun was shinning brightly but the air was still cool from the night. A feeling of gratitude filled my being. My time in Egypt was certainly blessed. In Cairo there was Shaker and Fula taking care of my every need. Then Safaa, not only allowing me to stay in her apartment, but taking care of all my travel arrangements. Now here I was on a luxury liner cruising down the Nile!

Being in Egypt was certainly an upgrade from the previous six months of my trip. I had been on a tight budget and was living very frugally. In Egypt it seemed that all the finer things in life were being placed in my path. I was content to sit back and enjoy every minute of it for as long as it lasted.

I met so many wonderful people on the ship and, as I suspected, they were all couples. But the people at my table during the meals and on the tours during the day were fun and friendly so I did not feel the least bit left out.

I bonded with an attractive lady from France who spoke English quite well. Her husband did not, so she and I spent a lot of time talking together. He liked taking afternoon naps so it worked out well. Another young couple from Greece was honeymooning. They had the same interest as I in exploring the ancient temples, buildings, and carvings on the tours along the way. We spent many hours together and were fast friends by the time the cruise was over. They gave me their address and phone number so I could call them when I reached Athens.

The meals on the ship were excellent. I consider myself a vegetarian, but I do eat fish, chicken, and turkey. After telling this to my waiter at the beginning of the cruise, I was served meals that were tasty and plentiful. The desserts were my downfall. I could not resist them so I put on a couple of pounds.

There was one mishap during the cruise. My camera stopped working! I realized it needed a new battery. I brought extra batteries with me from the United States, but they were safe in Cairo at Shaker's apartment. I finally found a man who was able to track one down. The battery cost three times as much as it was worth, but I had no choice but to pay the price. I could not be in Egypt amidst all these ancient ruins and not have photographs.

Toward the end of the cruise the crew planned a big party. We were all encouraged to dress in Egyptian attire. We women dressed in long dresses with scarves on our heads. The men wore Arabic headdresses and long capes. This attire is called "galabeya". The evening was to be an Egyptian dance celebration and the guests on the ship were encouraged to wear galabeya, which were available to rent in the gift shop.

I chose a long black dress with lots of beads and sequins on the bodice and a black scarf. After dressing, I walked to the gift shop and asked the proprietor to tie the scarf properly on my head. I was ready for the gala affair!

When I arrived in the dining room before the dance I noticed that the majority of the guests were dressed in Egyptian attire too. The tables for a special buffet dinner were filled with appetizing dishes attractively displayed. The food was in keeping with the Egyptian culture. The cuisine was simple but tasty. There were assortments of vegetables, legumes, green salads, and meat. The meat was typically veal or lamb. There were platters of rice and a flatbread called "baladi". The desserts consisted of rice pudding, baked pumpkin pie with no crust, and baked noodles with cream, nuts, and sweetness.

After our enormous feast, we moved upstairs to the bar for dancing. Egyptian dancing utilizes many of the moves employed by belly dancing, not easy for most of us. We all gave it the old college try and had a fantastic evening.

Usually the steward turned my bed down each evening. When I returned to my cabin that night, he had not only turned the bed down, he had also taken a pillow, dressed it in one of my t-shirts, and put an Arabic headdress on it. To complete his art work he added my sunglasses for a face. The phone receiver was propped next to the "face" as though it were talking on the phone. I had a good laugh before climbing into bed.

The next afternoon, while shopping in one of the many market places, I bought Egyptian headdresses as gifts for my son-in-law and my future son-in-law, a wonderful reminder of lovely days and nights cruising the Nile.

Upon returning to Cairo I was invited by Isis, Shaker's sister, to come to her home in Alexandria for a visit. I accepted her invitation. It was a pleasant two-and-half-hour train trip. When we arrived, Isis' housekeeper had a light lunch prepared for us. After lunch I explored her home and I was impressed with the antique furniture and the numerous artifacts filling the shelves.

Later Isis took me by car on a sightseeing tour. Alexandria is located on the northeastern coast of Egypt on the Mediterranean Sea. The seashore was glorious. We explored the lighthouse and the Montazah Palace, the summer residence of the royal family before the 1952 revolution. We came upon a group of school children about ten to twelve years of age. With smiles on their faces they spoke to me in Arabic. Isis said they wanted to have a photograph taken with me and wanted to know my name, where was I from, and how long would I be in Alexandria. A photograph was taken and then we said our good-byes and went on our way.

After stopping for tea, we went into the main part of Alexandria to shop. Isis took me to her special jeweler to look for gifts. I bought a cartouche for each of my daughters and one for myself. It is a pendant to be worn on a chain around one's neck. The name of the person is written in hieroglyphics. I thought it was the best gift to give as a memory of Egypt, and certainly the easiest to carry.

Isis drove me to the station for my return to Cairo by train. We hugged and said good-bye, not sure we would see each other again before I left Egypt in mid-April.

After returning to Cairo, I looked at my calendar and realized it was Easter Sunday in California. I called my oldest daughter. She and her husband were having an Easter egg hunt for my little granddaughter, now fourteen months old. I hung up the phone with pangs of sadness and loneliness for my family. The urge to cancel the rest of my trip and just pack up and go home was overwhelming. I was tired and missed my family so very much. But I still wanted to go to Israel, Greece, and other parts of Europe. I waited a few more days and decided I would continue on this adventure.

In early April the weather in Cairo changed abruptly. One day it was cool and suddenly it was warm followed by hot, dry weather. I thought Egypt was hot all year long and had been surprised by the chilly weather when I first arrived. This trip was not only teaching me about the culture of other countries, but also about geography and climate.

Israel had always been on my itinerary, but I had not given Jordan a thought until I reached Egypt. A number of people suggested I visit there as well. I could fly into Amman and take a bus to Petra, an ancient city that had once been under the sea, and was rediscovered and partially restored.

Safaa made my plane reservation. I paid for the ticket and found myself bound for Jordan.

Jordan

I had not been traveling on my own for a month. In Egypt my every wish was granted by loving friends. Now I was back on the road again and it felt a little scary.

That feeling was short-lived. When the plane landed, I claimed my luggage and took a taxi into town to a hotel suggested in my guide book. It was a relatively inexpensive room with four beds; I was the only occupant.

The next day I made arrangements with the Jett Bus Company for a trip to Petra. They had an opening on Sunday, the next day, so I booked a seat. I could also arrange with them for transportation to Israel.

A permit to leave Jordan was required and could be obtained at the Ministry of the Interior office. There is a three-day waiting period so I applied for that immediately.

All these things I learned as I traveled. I was not on a tour where everything was taken care of. Sometimes it was a pain to have to handle all the red tape, but I did like the freedom of staying longer in a place or leaving earlier if I so chose.

I took a day-trip to Jerash. As we drove through the city of Amman I noticed there was very little traffic congestion. Most of the buildings are white or cream-colored, giving it a neat and clean appearance.

As we reached the hilly, green countryside, I sat back in my seat to enjoy the pleasant ride. An hour later the bus stopped and the man next to me indicated that I was at my destination.

I stepped from the bus and saw a large archway. It was the beginning of the ruins in Jerash as described in my guide book. At the old Roman theater within the ruins site there were some local young men folk dancing. I watched them for a time.

I climbed the stairs to the top of the theater where I was treated to an overall view of the entire area. A Jordanian family spoke to me. They spoke little English so our conversation was limited. I was touched by their friendliness and efforts to converse with me. I found all the people to be gentle and friendly.

I located the restaurant, but was a little confused as the sign said "resting room". At first I thought it was the toilet but learned early on to investigate or ask questions, as things are usually different than they are at home.

I ordered hummus with pita bread and vegetable soup. It was delicious! I was liking Jordan better and better.

On Sunday morning I left Amman at 6:30 with a tour group aboard a Jett bus, destination Petra. Upon arriving we were met by Ahman, our guide for the day. He was an extremely attractive man in his early forties and had grown up in the area. He had a Master's degree in archeology and it was apparent that he loved his job. He seemed to put his heart and soul into sharing his vast knowledge with all of us.

To enter the old city we rode horses through a narrow passageway. I was astounded to learn that this old city had been underwater for 35,000 years! Some of you may be familiar with Petra. The movie "Indiana Jones and the Last Crusade" was filmed there.

Petra was the highlight of Jordan for me. It was probably one of the most fascinating places I had visited so far. If I ever return I will certainly plan on more than one day to explore this interesting area.

Israel

The next day I left by bus for the West Bank. It was not a smooth entry.

At the border there was not a problem getting through customs. On the other side taxis were waiting to transport us to Jerusalem. The drivers needed seven people per taxi before leaving.

The first group of people off the bus and through customs hired a taxi immediately. By the time my turn came, there was only one man remaining to share a taxi. We waited a while to see if anyone else would come. When that did not happen we were charged US$30 each.

Halfway to Jerusalem, the taxi driver, afraid to drive us all the way because he did not have Israeli license plates, stopped and we had to change taxis. In the hustle of transferring I almost left my camera and jacket on the seat. Luckily the man with me noticed them.

As we neared Jerusalem I could see the barbed wire fences and men in uniform with guns patrolling the fence. It was a very disconcerting feeling.

The taxi let us out at the Jaffa Gate at the Old City of Jerusalem, a central place for both of us. I picked up a map of Jerusalem at the tourist information office nearby. The clerk suggested the Bayit Bernstein Hostel, marking the way on the map. It was about a fifteen-minute uphill walk.

Finding the hostel without any trouble, I checked in and was shown to my room. It was a five-bed dormitory for $14.50 with breakfast included. The toilets and showers were on the floor above, not very convenient, but clean. The staff was surprisingly friendly. I decided to stay there for the night and try to reach a Servas member the next day. All my efforts to find other accommodations were in vain but as it turned out I really liked the hostel and the girls in my dorm.

I loved walking within the walls of the Old City; the Jewish Quarter, the Armenian Quarter, the Muslim Quarter, and the Western Wall.

The next day was Israel's Memorial Day. A great many people gathered at the Western Wall. The guide explained that the wall signifies where there once was a temple. It is believed if you stand close, touch it, and place a request to God on the Wall, the request will be answered. We were given time to do that. I was one of the first from our tour group to go forward. It was a peaceful experience.

We walked up the steps that are believed to be those that Jesus climbed with the cross on his back. We went to the church where the stones that covered the cave are kept. It was an informative and touching three hours.

Jerusalem was a little difficult to digest. Some of the people were very short-tempered and sometimes downright rude. The venders were pushy and became irritated if I tried to bargain. I guess I was spoiled by the friendliness in other countries. Here in Jerusalem I was just another tourist. These people were not treating me "special" as I had been treated in the past. Quickly I came to the conclusion that I may as well get used to that and also to the higher prices. Once I changed my attitude, all was well.

I visited the Holocaust Museum. The first section was the memorial to the 1.5 million children who died. It was a moving experience. I came out of there with tears in my eyes and sadness in my heart for all the pain suffered by the Jews at the hands of Hitler and his army. The rest of the museum was just as depressing.

I was more understanding of the people of Jerusalem after that tour. Their ancestors had gone through hell and some of that pain must still linger in the hearts of the younger generation.

The tour continued on to Bethlehem, the birthplace of Jesus. We visited the Church of the Nativity, built over the site of Jesus' birth. We were escorted into a basement-like cave of the church, the actual spot where Jesus was born. This was a truly spiritual experience for me and I felt the presence of the Son of the Creator.

When I returned to the hostel I met all of my roommates. We were an international group. Christina from France, Sanda from Slovenia, Elizabeth from Austria, and Heidi from Germany. We made plans to dine together. Since it was the eve of Israel

Independence Day, there would be a big celebration that evening with dancing in the streets. We all wanted to join in the festivities.

We ate dinner at an outdoor cafe and then wandered through the streets filled with people tooting horns and throwing streamers in celebration of their independence. On King George Street, a live band played while the people enjoyed folkdancing. We stood on the sidelines to watch and shortly were invited to join in. What fun it was to be in Jerusalem dancing in the streets with the locals.

The curfew at the hostel was 12:00 midnight. We made it with only ten minutes to spare. Soon we heard the sounds of fireworks and we all ran up to the roof to watch. What a wonderful evening we had, enjoying a traditional celebration in Israel.

The next day Sanda and I took a bus tour to the Dead Sea. First we went to Masada, to see the fortress of Herod the Great. On the way the bus drove on a road alongside the Dead Sea, which is 399 feet below sea level; Masada is at sea level.

Before taking the elevator 400 feet up to the fortress, we stopped at a gift shop. On all tours in any country I visited there was always a gift shop stop for the tourist to spend money. Israel was no exception.

This shop had many skin products made from the minerals and salts of the Dead Sea. I purchased face cream, night cream, body lotion, and some bath salts. I read in my guide book that their products were of the best quality and beneficial for the skin. After basking in the sun for so many months, I knew my skin could use some help.

Following our shopping spree we took the elevator to the top, to the fortress of Masada. We enjoyed the expansive views while the guide supplied information about the remains of the fortress built by Herod. However, with being hard of hearing, I didn't hear much of his talk.

Down the steep incline we went, and we were back on the bus and on our way to the Dead Sea. Neither Sanda nor I had bathing suits, but we did have t-shirts, which we put on in the dressing room.

Floating in the Dead Sea! What a great experience! The salt content is ten times greater than any other body of water and you cannot sink. I accidentally splashed some water into my mouth and it had a horrible taste. The water is not only saline but also oily, giving it a very black, murky look. We asked a man standing nearby to take a photograph of us floating in the dark, salty water.

Near the dressing rooms, in an area where you can smear black mud on for a "black mud bath," we ran into Christina, our room-mate from France. We rubbed the black mud on each other, taking photographs of the event. After the mud was on, the idea was to let it dry to remove the impurities of the body. Unfortunately, we were running out of time. Our bus was leaving soon so we had a quick shower to remove the mud. Our t-shirts were stained a gray color from the oily sea and the black mud. They ended up in a garbage can.

My last evening in Jerusalem, our international group of women went out for a farewell dinner. We all exchanged addresses. Sanda and Elizabeth invited me to come to visit them. I wanted to visit Austria but I wasn't sure about Slovenia. In fact, I had never heard of the country until I met Sanda. She explained that it was formerly a part of Yugoslavia, located in the northeastern corner, surrounded by Italy and Austria.

We said our good-byes that night. I got up early the next morning to go to the central bus station for transportation back to Egypt. I promised to keep in touch with the girls and let them know if and when I was coming to visit.

Back in Cairo

The trip back to Cairo was long and uneventful. Returning to this congested, smog-polluted city was not pleasant. The air had been so clean and pure in Jordan and Israel.

I was leaving Cairo in a few days so I had business that needed attention. I wanted to change my airline reservations from Cairo to Athens instead of flying into Zurich as scheduled.

I went to Delta Airlines, the main carrier from my around-the-world ticket and found I would have to pay an extra $300.00 to make that change. I charged the fare to my Visa card. I also purchased a Eurail pass from the Thomas Cook Co, a large travel agency. I did not buy that in the United States because one must use the pass within six months of purchase. With these two important items handled, I turned my attention toward putting a package together to mail home. I packed a box with personal things no longer needed for the remainder of my travels as well as treasured gifts from Egypt, Jordan, and Israel.

My last night in Cairo, Safaa and I went to one of her favorite Indian restaurants for dinner. That was appropriate since we had met in India.

After a month in Egypt I was glad to be going on. The weather had warmed up and it was very hot, and the smog was horrible. Even the noise level seemed to have risen in the traffic-congested streets. I knew I would never complain about Los Angeles smog again. The traffic and congestion there is mild compared to Cairo!

Meeting and spending time with Safaa and becoming re-acquainted with Shaker after all those years was delightful. I was not able to say a formal good-bye to Shaker as he was away on business when I returned from Israel, but I sent him a thank-you note. His kindness and friendly hospitality still remain in my heart.

I am still in touch with Safaa via email and a few years ago she came to Los Angeles and I drove up to spend time with her. I also keep in touch with Asaad, but I have not heard from Shaker for quite a while.

Greece

My plane landed in Athens at 10:00 in the morning. I went through the normal routine—passport check, money changing, and picking up my backpack. Then I asked at the information desk the quickest and cheapest way into the city. The clerk pointed in the direction of the express bus stand.

The girl with whom I sat on the bus was going to the same hotel. She had stayed there before and knew exactly where to get off and which direction to go. Was that luck? I think it was just the Universe taking care of me once again.

After checking into the Festos Hotel, I discovered it was ideally located near the tourist office, the post office, and the main shopping area. The shopping area is called the Phlaka or flea market. It is filled with shops, good restaurants, and fun cafes.

I airmailed my exposed film to California from the post office in Athens for the equivalent of four American dollars.

At the tourist office I picked up a ferry schedule for travel from Athens to the Greek Islands. Another dream was about to materialize!

I walked the short distance to the Phlaka, which was more like a bazaar than a flea market. I found a nice outdoor cafe, sat down, and ordered a Greek salad, of course. Bread came with it.

The Phlaka is located at the foot of the Acropolis. After eating I found the path leading up to this magnificent complex. From that vantage point the view of Athens is fabulous.

This was not an advantageous time of day for photographs as the sun was not at the correct angle. I did not go into the ruins of the Acropolis at that time. I would come back during the morning hours to enjoy the ruins and take photographs. The next few hours were spent exploring Athens. It seemed rather quiet compared to the noise of Cairo.

After reading my guide book I decided to spend only that night in Athens and go immediately to the Islands. I could explore Athens and others parts of Greece later on.

I left the next morning on the Apollo II Express Ferry enroute to Paros Island, the first of my Greek Island trips. On the five-hour ferry ride over, I had plenty of time to scan my guide book for inexpensive places to stay. I decided upon the Pension Lido. It was well located on the island and the price was right.

As I walked down the gangplank, a man stopped me and asked if I needed accommodations. I said I was looking for Pension Lido and he said, "That's my place. Just follow me." Again I was taken care of without any effort on my part.

My room was neat and clean with a private bath and even the bonus of a small balcony, all for only $10.28 per night, if I stayed three nights. This was not the prime season so the prices were down.

I was still having problems with my camera. Even with the new battery it was sluggish and now it was making a strange sound when I opened the lens. At a camera shop I was told that there was a problem with the lens but I could continue to use it to capture the lovely island on film.

During lunch at an outdoor cafe I met a young girl from Australia. She was looking for a summer job. Many people I met along the way took jobs to replenish their finances in order to continue their travels. After talking for a time, we made plans to meet for dinner.

Meeting new and interesting people is the real benefit of traveling alone. I met people much more readily than I would have if I had been with a companion. Some of them were much younger than I, as was this young lady. She was only 25 but we related well. In fact, we had a very enjoyable evening together. I think she, more than I, was completely blown away that she could have so much fun with someone so much older. I am sure she had never sat with her mother and giggled as we did that evening.

The next day I picked up a map of the island of Paros from the tourist information office and went to explore Santa Maria Beach. This is the wind surfers' beach. However, since it was off season, no one was there.

I sat on the sand and looked around. Rocks, lovely beach, blue, blue water and off in the distance, small white houses with a few trees completed the picture. I felt peaceful.

"Have I died and gone to heaven?" I asked myself. The only thing missing from this perfect picture was my "Greek God" to keep me company.

And while I am on the subject of a Greek God, I must say I was disappointed in the Greek men. I am not sure what I was expecting, but the short, squat, mostly plump men were not what I fantasized.

I also found them extremely loud. To get a point across, many of the men shouted and gestured wildly with their hands. Many times I thought this was anger only to find they were enthusiastically expressing themselves.

After a few more days on the small island, I boarded a ferry to Santorini. This island looked like a huge rock in the middle of the sea. From a distance I thought it was snowcapped. A closer view revealed it had all-white buildings and houses nestled on the rocks.

On the bus ride from the ferry dock to the main town of Fira, we drove along the cliff's edges before heading inland. At the bus stop in Fira there was a gentleman waiting, hoping to escort any takers to his small hotel. Sandra, a girl I met on the ferry, and I decided to follow him to check out the rooms.

The hotel was about a half-mile walk, mostly uphill. We arrived panting and sweating. Pleased with the rooms, we checked in. The owner showed us a shortcut to the main area for shopping and eating.

The island of Santorini was fascinating. A walkway followed along the ridge of the town, overlooking the sea. It seemed to stretch for miles. The path went up and down and, around each bend, we had another incredible view of the shimmering blue Aegean Sea below. I was told that Santorini has an area of approximately 28 square miles.

In this inner section of Fira there were no cars. The walkways are for pedestrians or little carts pulled by small donkeys. Most of the buildings are white with blue roofs or domes.

The island was once a volcano, and the beaches on Santorini are all black sand. This is an awesome contrast to the normal white sandy beach. However, in the heat of the summer I understand it becomes so hot it is impossible to walk on the beach without shoes. A bamboo pad, or something heavier than a towel, would be needed to lie on the hot sand.

Further exploration took me to the village of Oia, situated on the northern tip of Santorini Island. It is the first village that you see as you arrive by ferry. Numerous homes are carved out of the sides of the rocks. It was very quiet because I was there during the off-season. The owners of the restaurants and bars were busy painting and cleaning to prepare for the onslaught of tourists in the coming weeks.

It was late April and a bit chilly. Even during the day when I was in the sun, it felt cool. At night I always appreciated a wrap.

I left Santorini Island thinking that I would like to return someday. It was so beautiful, romantic, and friendly. I enjoyed it alone, but because of its romantic beauty I at times felt lonely, even when I had dinner with Sandra. If God ever blesses me with the love of my life, I would like to return with him to Santorini Island.

The Island of Naxos was my next stop. I found a small but clean hotel near the center of town. After checking in, I met a young man from England. Our small verandahs connected. He shared his map of Naxos with me.

Later in the village, while I sipped a cup of tea and wrote postcards, Mike, my new friend from England, joined me. After talking for a while, I excused myself to go to the beach. He asked if I'd like to join him for dinner that evening. I told him I would be delighted and off I went.

It was warmer on Naxos Island. In a short time I was very warm so I walked out to the water to cool off. It was freezing! In spite of the coldness I plunged in. Never having been in the Aegean Sea, I did not let this opportunity pass. In a few moments my body was numb so I stayed and enjoyed myself. When I came out of the water my skin was tingling and I felt invigorated. I stretched out in the sun to thaw.

That evening Mike and I walked the short distance into the village. We stopped at a cafe for tea and to decide where we might like to have dinner. The restaurant he suggested would not open for another half-hour so we walked to the end of the street as the sun was setting. It was one of the prettiest sunsets I have ever seen. We sat on a bench admiring the lovely view, silently enjoying one another's company.

At the restaurant Mike ordered for both of us. We had Greek style potato salad, regular Greek salad and calamari. The meal was served family style with lots of olive oil and herbs. What a scrumptious meal!

Mike ferried on to another island later that night. I said good-bye to him at the dock. We exchanged cards. When I returned from my travels I had postcards from him. Another benefit of traveling. But I don't receive very many cards and letters from friends I met all over the world anymore. Too many years have passed, and life marches on.

The next day, tired from many hours of exploring more of the island, I was informed by the owner of my hotel that I would have to vacate my room. He had 20 people coming in from Athens, and because it was a large party he needed my room.

I could not believe he asked me to leave without prior notice, but he did. He did help me find another room, but it was small and shabby. I did not feel comfortable in the new location so I decided to go on to Mykonos Island the next day.

To make an uncomfortable situation even worse, the weather changed. High winds came up, making a crossing to Mykonos on the Flying Dolphin, the express boat, impossible. Unless a miracle happened and the winds died down during the night, I would have to cross on the large ferry to Paros and then change to another ferry to get to Mykonos.

The next morning the winds had not ceased but seemed to be blowing even stronger. I still wanted to leave, so I boarded the ferry bound for Paros.

I had a six-hour wait on the island of Paros in the chilly, windy weather. The time went relatively fast and before long, I was back on the ferry. We were scheduled to arrive on Mykonos at 10:00 that night. I did not have a room booked but trusted that someone with budget accommodations would meet the ferry. I was right.

I chose a very pleasant Greek lady who offered a room in my price range. She and her son drove me to the Zannis Hotel. It was on a hill within walking distance of the city center.

My room was very nice. It had a small bed, night stand, dresser with mirror, a couple of chairs, and a private bath. When one is traveling on a budget, having a private bath is always a bonus. Another bonus in this small but quaint hotel was the patio. There was a lovely view of the ocean, which all the rooms faced.

I was excited about being on Mykonos, known as the island for the jetsetters. After being on the other quiet islands I was in the mood for more people and a little noise. It was May first and still early for the «season», but it was Easter Sunday in Greece, so there were more people on this island than all the others put together. The Greek Orthodox celebrate Easter a few weeks later than we do.

The wind was still blowing. Luckily the sun was shining brightly or it would have been really cold. Because of the wind, all boat trips were canceled. I was disappointed that I would not get to visit the Island of Delos. According to mythology, Delos was the birthplace of Apollo, the god of light, poetry, music, and healing. Delos can only be visited, you cannot stay overnight on the island. The boat schedule allows a three-hour visit and it is suggested that you bring plenty of water and food as the cafeteria is a rip-off.

By the end of the day I had seen enough of Mykonos. Because of the weather I could not go to Delos, which was one of the big attractions for me, nor did I have a desire to travel to any of the beaches with the wind blowing so fiercely. I checked on the ferry schedule for crossing to Athens the next morning; then I wandered over to the windmills, the big tourist attraction on Mykonos.

At a sidewalk cafe I almost walked into the pink pelican. I thought this was a myth but now I knew that the stories of the pink pelican were actually true. He stood right in front of me! Quickly I snapped a couple of photographs. The huge pelican, about three feet tall, roams the streets of Mykonos completely free. The pink pelican has been a tradition there since 1954. If you visit Mykonos you will most likely see one.

Back in Athens, I checked in with the Festos Hotel long enough to leave my bags, then boarded a bus to Delphi, a town near the central part of Greece. It is about three hours from Athens and in the mountains.

I called the youth hostel from the bus station in Delphi and was given directions to their location. It was up a very steep hill, but luckily my large bag was in Athens and my small daypack was relatively light. I was glad my legs were in fairly fit condition from all the trudging up and down the hills of Santorini and Mykonos, but I was still tired when I reached the hostel. My room had four beds but I was the only occupant at the moment. It had a balcony with a panoramic view overlooking the town, the valley, the mountains, and a body of water that I thought was a lake but found out later was actually the Gulf of Corinth.

After lunch I walked to Ancient Delphi. The city was closed but I continued on and found the Temple of Athena in a serene, comfortable setting. I struck up a conversation with a lady and her nephew from the United States. We sat there talking and enjoying the peacefulness for more than an hour. My two new friends were staying at the hostel as well. We made plans to meet for dinner.

When I returned to my room I had a roommate, Maggie, a young Australian lady now living in England. We took a bus to visit the nearby ski resort of Arochova. It was a foggy day so the views were not what we had hoped they would be. The town was having an athletic event so we watched the young men participate in a running and jumping contest. We never did find out what it was all about.

The weather was cool and slightly windy, but nothing like the wind on the islands. Then it began to rain; to get out of it we stopped for a cup of tea and a "potty break" before taking the bus back to Delphi.

The rain continued so I decided to return to Athens. While packing my daypack I realized my camera was gone. I remembered hanging it on the coat hook in the stall of the bathroom when we had tea in Arochova. I must have left it behind! As I boarded the bus for Athens, I asked the driver if I could get off in Arochova for a few minutes to see if my camera had been turned in at the cafe. He said they always stop there anyway.

Well, I guess it was time for me and my camera to part. It was not there.

I found out later that the last two rolls of exposed film were scratched. The problem with the lens had affected the quality of my photographs. When I learned that, I felt better about having to purchase a new camera in Athens.

I bought a new Fuji point-and-shoot camera for about US$285, which was approximately the price I had paid for my lost one. I left the store with my new camera and browsed in the flea market. A postcard of the pink pelican caught my eye. I heard a male voice with an accent say, "He really is there on the Island of Mykonos." I turned and smiled at a tall red-haired man and said, "Yes, I know. I took a photo of him very similar to this one." I moved on to other postcards.

About twenty minutes later, as I turned a corner to enter a shop, I bumped into someone. When I glanced up to say, "Excuse me," I was looking into the green eyes of the red-haired man who had spoken to me before. We both laughed and I said, "Are you following me?" He laughed and asked if he could buy a cold drink for me. I accepted.

We found seats at an outdoor cafe nearby. He ordered two Fanta orange sodas. His name was Alexandrios and he was born and raised in Athens. He was the captain of a charter boat that cruises the Greek Islands.

The conversation turned to astrological signs and we found that ours was Taurus. His birthday is May 19 and mine is May 6, which was the next day. Being born in the same month is where the similarities ended. He would be 38 on his birthday and I would be 57 on mine! I did not share my age with him.

It was hard for me to believe that I was that age. Why, I still felt as though I was 38. I guess Alexandrios didn't notice the age difference, or if he did, he did not mind, because he invited me to spend the evening of my birthday with him. I agreed, so we made plans for him to meet me at my hotel at 4:00 the next afternoon.

I looked forward to spending my birthday evening with a friend instead of being alone.

Early the next day I walked to the Acropolis once again. It was an opportune time for photographs of this magnificent area. I purchased my ticket and roamed through the ruins. Then I walked to the top of Philapappou Hill. From that viewpoint, I had a panoramic view of Athens and the Acropolis.

I was in the lobby when Alexandrios arrived promptly at 4:00.

"I have something special planned for your birthday," he announced.

We set out on foot. I tried to coax him into telling me where we were going. He just smiled and said, "Follow me."

We walked about 15 minutes and then he stopped in front of a very nice apartment building. As he turned to escort me to the front door, I stopped and said, "Wait a minute. Where are we?"

"This is my apartment I share with a friend. I stay here when I am in Athens."

"I am sorry Alexandrios, but I cannot go to your apartment."

"But I have prepared a special Greek meal for you. It is ready and waiting for us to eat," he said with pride in his voice.

I stood there a few moments. What was I to do? I did not want to put myself in jeopardy, but I also did not want to offend this man if his intentions were honorable. I decided to trust him. He was a perfect gentleman the day before and I felt comfortable with him.

We took an elevator to his second floor small, neat, clean apartment. True to his word, a small table in front of the sofa was set with place mats, napkins, and silverware for two. He motioned for me to sit down, excusing himself to go to the kitchen. He returned shortly with a tray. Two plates contained fresh green beans with garlic and olive oil. He also served fresh tzatziki, a popular Greek dip made with yogurt, cucumber and garlic. He proudly told me he had made the tzatziki himself. I was impressed. It was delicious.

He wished me a happy birthday saying, "How old are you? "About 45?"

I smiled and replied, "A little older than that." He didn't probe further, just told me his last girlfriend was 42.

We had a delightful time talking and eating. After the marvelous meal he showed me photographs of his boat. It was beautiful—125 feet, a real yacht! Then he turned on the music and taught me Greek folk dancing. It was fun to be dancing and laughing.

When we sat down to rest he brought out a photograph album of his family and friends. He was proud to show me photographs of his mom, an attractive redhead. He proudly announced that she was 58 years old!

Upon hearing that, the reality of our age difference hit me. Before he entertained any amorous ideas I decided to tell him the truth about my age. I confessed. He was shocked and kept saying, "But I thought you were in your 40s."

Apparently he decided the age difference didn't matter because he put his arm around me to pull me close. I said, "No,

Alexandrios, let's just keep this a friendship." Of course that upset his male Greek ego.

He retorted with, "I thought you were as attracted to me as I am to you."

I sat there knowing I had made a big mistake. I had willingly gone to his apartment. It was not the right thing for me to do, going to the apartment of a man I had just met. I wasn't a naive young girl, I knew the ropes. I should have known he might be interested in more than just idle conversation. I knew I was to blame. I apologized for misleading him, thanked him for a lovely meal, then rose and walked to the door. He let me leave without expressing any bitterness or ill feelings.

I had been lonely. It was my birthday and I did not want to spend it alone. Instead of making the wisest decision I had let my romantic heart get in the way. I was thousands of miles from home, in a foreign country, and traveling alone. I had taken a risk I shouldn't have. That was a valuable lesson for me to learn. I am a lucky lady that it turned out so well.

The last few days in Athens I took time to shop, to mail a package home, and confirm my flight from Athens to Zurich, Switzerland. After three attempts I found a Servas host in Zurich, who would be pleased to have me stay with her. I would be there for only a few days. My two-month Eurail trip began in Zurich.

Switzerland

I arrived in Zurich on May 9, 1994 after traveling almost eight months. I was tired, but now that I had arrived in a new country with yet another language, another money exchange, and unfamiliar customs, I found myself eager for the experience.

I called Denise, my Servas host, from the airport. She told me to take a train to downtown Zurich, then gave me directions to her apartment via the local tram system. I arrived at the downtown train station about noon. Denise would not be home from work until after 5:00 that afternoon, so I checked my bag in a locker at the train station and went exploring.

Even though it was drizzling rain when I left the train station, the air was clean. There was little congestion from traffic. Most people ride the train, bus, or the tram system to and from the city.

I liked Zurich immediately, but it was obvious that the days of inexpensive meals and lodging were over. I found Switzerland to be one of the more expensive countries in Europe.

When I met my hostess, Denise, I found her friendly and helpful. Her apartment was small but comfortable. She had a futon on the living room floor for me to sleep on. That was fine with me. I was used to sleeping on any type of bed.

I stayed in Zurich two nights and then activated my Eurail pass. First destination was Nice, France.

The train left Zurich in the early morning. It was clean and comfortable, with large windows that enabled me to view the countryside. A welcome contrast to the trains in India. I settled back and relaxed. After all these months of thinking about it and talking about it, I was now actually beginning my excursion around Europe.

I had been to Europe twice before, many years ago. I had seen Zurich, but it looked different to me this time. Now I was on my way to Nice. I had been there as well but had little recollection of it.

The train ride through Switzerland was captivating, with views of gigantic, rugged, snow-capped mountains. The rivers and waterfalls further enhanced the magnificent scenery.

It was a long trip with a change of trains in Milan, Italy. What a difference! Gone was the nice, clean, comfortable train. This one was old and uncomfortable. There was also a change in the terrain. Gone were the beautiful mountains and waterfalls. Now all I saw were empty fields that seemed to stretch for miles.

Then, thank God, the landscape changed abruptly. I was traveling along the coast. The Italian Riviera was beautiful. I changed trains again in Ventimiglia, Italy, on the border with France.

France

As the train traveled along the French Riviera, I felt excited. We passed Monaco, then Èze. The next stop was mine. Nice, France!

It was 6:00 in the evening and I had been traveling for twelve long hours. I quickly disembarked the train, changed money into French francs, and located a map at the tourist office. The night before I had called from Zurich for a hotel reservation. The Hotel Belle Meuniere was only a block from the train station.

My room contained four beds with a shared bathroom. There was a small balcony overlooking the courtyard. I paid $18 per night which included a continental breakfast.

The first night my roommates were all guys. This had happened to me a number of times in my travels. The first time I was a little surprised, but now I just accepted it as normal. Two of them checked out the next morning, leaving me and a fellow from Germany. We both knew the other two beds would be full by that evening.

After getting settled, I walked down to the courtyard and joined my roommate and other guests of the hotel. I learned I was very lucky to have a room. The Grand Prix car races had started their preliminary runs in Monte Carlo that day, and the French Film Festival was in Cannes. I could not believe I was there in time to enjoy both of these famous events! Once again I was being divinely guided by a powerful source.

The Promenade des Anglais overlooks Nice's beach. I sat on a bench and looked out in wonder at the Mediterranean Sea. The sky was overcast but it was still a spectacular sight. Perhaps just the thought of being on the French Riviera had something to do with my state of euphoria.

I have always kidded my daughters about their working hard so they could take care of me some day while I lived on the French Riviera. That thought now brought a smile to my face. Maybe I had not been kidding.

I loved the time I spent on the French Riviera. I enjoyed exploring Nice by sitting in an outdoor cafe and looking up at the lovely verandas filled with beautiful greenery and flowers. I took the train to Monaco and watched trials of the races. I visited the Palace in time to see the changing of the guard and I walked to the casino but did not go in because I was in shorts.

The day of the Grand Prix race I went back to Monaco. I did not have tickets to see the race but took photographs of the crowds. I stopped for a dish of ice cream and watched the race on television. I could hear the roaring sounds of the cars from the open door. Being in Monaco at Grand Prix time was very exciting!

I took the train to Cannes a couple of times. As mentioned, the French Film Festival was in progress. Clint Eastwood was the host that year, but I never even got a glimpse of him. I walked around Cannes, standing in the crowds, trying in vain to glimpse someone famous whom I might recognize.

Many years ago I visited Nice with a friend. While we were there she visited a little village called Eze. I had been unable to go along because I did not feel well from eating some bad fish the night before. For all these many years I promised myself if I ever returned I would go to Eze, because my friend had raved about it. Now that opportunity presented itself.

I took the train from Nice and got off at the Eze station. At a tobacco shop I asked for directions to the village situated on a hill high above. Luckily, in areas where there are numerous tourists, most of the French people speak some English. I walked in the direction indicated by the clerk and came upon a sign and an arrow that read "village." I followed the arrow and found a path and a sign that read, "Eze Village 358 meters". Off I went.

Three-quarters of the way up I could see a magnificent chateau nestled on the edge of the cliff. That majestic scene was a tremendous inspiration to keep going. Tired and thirsty, I finally reached the top where I found the most fascinating village.

Walking up and down hills, I browsed through the many shops. The more I walked, the more shops I discovered tucked away in corners of this large, ancient chateau. Hot, tired, and ravenous, I chose a quaint-looking restaurant overlooking the sea far below. I was fatigued, but after reaching the top I felt every tiring step had been worth the opportunity to experience these superb views, charming shops, and delicious food. However, I did not walk back down. I stretched my budget and hired a taxi to return to the train station.

I adapted easily to the lifestyle of the French Riviera. A part of me wanted to linger there longer, but other wondrous places were on my itinerary. It was time to venture on.

Italy

I arrived in Florence on a late afternoon train. Making my way to the information desk for a city map and getting money changed were relatively easy in the Santa Maria Nevella train station. The lady at the information desk told me where to find the bus to the Ostella Hostel. My reservation for a bed had been confirmed with a phone call from Nice.

I loved Florence from the moment I arrived. It is old and somewhat dreary-looking at first, but as I looked deeper, I discovered that the charm of Florence can be found in its history and tradition. It is a city rich in art, culture, and history.

I visited most of the must-see places listed in my guide book. Just walking the streets of Florence is much like visiting an art museum. I walked for hours, stopping often for photographs. It rained most of the time I was there. Even the rain and overcast skies did not detract from the beauty and charm of this enchanting city.

I did not find Florence overly expensive, except for the gelato. When I ordered a chocolate gelato cone, I was shocked to hear that it cost 12,000 lire, which was at that time over seven American dollars, almost the same price as my room at the hostel!

From Florence I took the train to Venice. The weather improved—no rain and the sun was shining, with only a few clouds in the sky.

I found a room in an all-women hostel on the Grand Canal of Venice. I reached the hostel aboard a vaporette, a small ferry boat, much like a taxi, that is used for transportation on the canals.

After checking into the hostel, I took a vaporette over to San Marcus Square, which is the most popular place to visit in Venice. The square is known for its thousands of pigeons just waiting to be fed.

The secret to really explore Venice is to walk. I wandered for hours down narrow streets that line the small canals, taking photographs of gondolas transporting couples. I could feel romance all around me. One does not need a lover to feel romantic in this glorious city.

After hours on my feet, I stopped for a cup of tea. I was sitting quietly, absorbing all I had seen, when a lady at the table next to mine struck up a conversation. She had been traveling for only two weeks and was already lonely and unsure of what to do next. After listening to her fears, indecisions, and complaints for about a half-hour I made an excuse and left.

I guess it does take a certain type of person to travel, especially alone. One must be confident, most of the time, in one's judgments, and one must be comfortable being alone. It helps to be spontaneous and flexible, and patience helps too. Visiting cultures that are so different from your own can be trying. Just being open to another way of doing things can make or break a trip.

A few days later I decided it was time to leave Venice. I called Benadetta, one of my roommates at the ashram in India, who had invited me to visit her when I reached Italy. She lives in a small town not too far from Venice. After many weeks of traveling by train I was tired, so a few days visiting a friend in a small town sounded like the tonic I needed.

When she knew it was I on the phone she sounded delighted that I was coming to visit her. She told me which train to take from Venice, saying she would be at the station to meet me.

While still in Venice I wrote a note to the two girls I met in Israel, Sanda from Slovenia and Elizabeth in Austria. After my visit with Benadetta, I was thinking about going on to these two countries. I wasn't completely sure about Slovenia. Sanda did not have a phone and she might have moved from the address that I had for her. She told me that the town in which she lived was very small and if she did move, anyone there would know her new address. Even with this assurance I could still feel the fear take hold every time I thought about going to this strange country. I had never even heard of Slovenia until I met Sanda.

I said to myself, "I won't think about it until the time comes, then I will decide."

Benadetta met me at the train station. She was as I remembered - a tall, attractive Italian lady with a ready smile and a friendly disposition. Her home was located on a grand estate owned by the family. Her mother lived in the large, main house. She and other brothers and sisters lived in smaller homes within the estate grounds. Benadetta lived in a small, attractive three-bedroom, which she shared with her boyfriend and her teenage daughter.

The estate is over 5,000 years old, and has been in the family for generations. Being there in that lovely setting was a real treat after having lived in dormitories since leaving Switzerland.

Fatigued from traveling, I felt a cold coming on. At a local pharmacy I purchased vitamin C and replaced the garlic capsules that I had run out of recently. Garlic is a natural antibiotic, and I had been taking it since the beginning of my travels. I believe the garlic helped keep me healthy while I traveled. A short rest was just what I needed before continuing on.

When I shared my dilemma about going to Slovenia with Benadetta, she said to me, "You have been traveling to strange countries for the last number of months. What is different this time? If you do not find your friend, you get a hotel room for the night, look around, and leave."

How simple. All I needed was a little encouragement from a friend. She was right. Of course I would go. Why miss an opportunity such as this?

Benadetta is one of the nicest, kindest, and most giving people I have met. She gave so freely, and I don't mean material things, but warmth from the very depth of her heart. She was so tender and touchy with her daughter and her boyfriend. When she talked about her siblings she only said very complimentary things. She is truly an Angel of God. She offered to drive me to the Slovenia border but I declined. It was an an hour and a half drive and I did not want to impose on my friend any longer. I chose to take the train.

The cold I seemed to be getting just a few short days before was gone. Now that I felt better I was eager for the adventure. I was rested and energetic as I boarded the train to Gorizia, a town near the Italy-Slovenia border.

Slovenia

It was both scary and exciting to be off on this excursion. I was not sure where I was going or if I would find Sanda when I got there, but I knew from past experience that all I needed to do was just relax and let this adventure unfold.

My guides and helpers were with me from the moment I stepped off the train in Gorizia, Italy.

I asked a lady how to reach Nova Gorica, the town immediately across the border in Slovenia. I took Bus No. 3, asking the driver to let me off at the border. As I stepped off the bus I saw a sign that read "Welcome to Slovenia." Hoisting my backpack, I bravely walked up to the border guard. He looked at my passport, stamped it, waved me on, and I walked across the border!

Directly in front of me was an information booth. Next to it was a place where I changed money into Slovenian currency. I then asked how to get a bus to the town of Deskle. I was told to go into the city center and take a bus from the Nova Gorica bus station.

I walked across the street to a bus stop and discovered I could not read the sign. Not knowing which bus to take, I stood there trying to figure out what to do, when a man walked up. He greeted me in his native language and I told him I only spoke English. Much to my amazement, he responded in English! His English was broken but understandable. I related my dilemma and he said he was taking the bus that would pass by the bus station I wanted to reach. He motioned for me to join him on the bus that had just arrived.

He indicated when I needed to get off. I thanked him, stepped from the bus, and walked toward the bus station. The ticket lady did not understand English, but when I wrote the word "Deskle" she sold me a ticket and pointed to a bus leaving immediately.

I ran the short distance and climbed aboard an already full bus. I had only enough room to stand on the step by the door with my backpack. A young girl took my small daypack to hold in her lap. I asked her if the bus was going to Deskle. In English she answered, "Yes," and added that she would tell me when to get off.

A girl next to her spoke to me in English saying she was getting off at Deskle too. I handed her a paper with Sanda's address on it and she said she would take me there when we arrived.

It came as a pleasant surprise that so many people in Slovenia spoke English.

In about a half-hour we reached the small town of Deskle. The girl walked with me the short distance to a two-story apartment building. I was not sure what to expect. Had Sanda moved and would the people in the apartment building know where she had moved to?

I knocked on the door and it was opened by a giant! The man towered over me. I judged him to be six-feet, six-inches tall. My young guardian spoke to him in their native tongue and he began smiling from ear to ear saying, "Yes, yes, please come in. Sanda be home soon!"

I thanked the young lady and followed the nice man into the small apartment. He was Boris, Sanda's boyfriend. They lived there together. He told me in broken English that Sanda was out and would be home in the late afternoon. He invited me to sit down and went into the kitchen and busied himself at the stove. A few minutes later he was back and said, "Lunch is ready."

I was in for a treat. Boris had prepared a tasty tofu soup, served with brown rice and cauliflower. And, as is the custom in Greece and Italy, he offered olive oil and lemon to flavor the rice. As an added treat he provided sesame seeds to sprinkle on top. He was a great cook; I ate every bite.

His healthy eating habits came as a surprise to me. From spending time with Sanda in Israel, I knew she ate meat and also smoked. Boris was the exact opposite, a vegetarian and a non-smoker.

After lunch he took me for a drive to the Soco River. We stopped and hiked on a trail along the river's edge. We were gone for about two hours. Sanda still wasn't home when we returned.

Boris was a physical education teacher at the local high school, so he left me alone while he went to basketball practice. I would like to have gone out to explore the little town, but not having a key to the apartment, I could not leave. About 8:30 that evening, as I sat on the verandah reading, I heard a car horn honk. Looking down, I saw Sanda smiling and waving at me as she drove around the corner. Sanda was pleased to see me, apologizing for being so late. There was no need for an apology. She had not known which day or what time I might arrive.

Sanda worked as a dealer in a casino from 8:00 in the morning until 8:00 in the evening most days. Boris went to work at 8:00 and was home by 1:00 in the afternoon. In Sanda's absence, Boris appointed himself my tour guide. Each afternoon we drove to another fascinating place. We visited the Postojna Caves. There were 26 kilometers of caves but only five kilometers were open to the public then. We took a train ride down into the caves and then walked with a guide. It was quite cold down there but Boris, thinking of my welfare, brought a heavy jacket for me.

Boris had a passion for old castles. I was thrilled as I had always had a burning desire to explore old castles myself. Occasionally as we drove along, we'd see a castle in the distance and find our way to the entrance and roam around the grounds.

Sanda took a few days off from work, because she wanted to spend some time with me and show me some parts of her country.

She grew up in Koper, a small town located near the coast of the Adriatic Sea. On our visit to Koper, Sanda's sister joined us for a sightseeing tour of a number of other nearby towns.

No one would ever take these two girls for sisters; they looked nothing alike. They are about the same height, but Sanda has dark hair and dark eyes and an olive complexion. Her sister is very blond, with fair skin and blue eyes.

On our excursion, my favorite place was Piran. It is an old, quaint town set on a point at the end of the Istrian Peninsula. It is built in the style of Venetian architecture.   We chose an out-door cafe for lunch to better enjoy the lovely day and the beauty of the coastline. We ordered a huge platter filled with a variety of fresh fish, and ate leisurely. When I asked for the check the waiter said it had already been taken care of. I objected. I planned this to be my opportunity to repay my hosts for their hospitality. Sanda would not hear of it!

Later that day we ventured across the border into Croatia. Sanda said not to worry as this was a safe area. I trusted my friend's judgement. We drove an hour and a half to the town of Zonenj. I was tired of being in the car all day, but once we arrived it was well worth the effort. It is an old, rustic, charming town jutting out into the sea. As you look out into the water, you can see other islands in the distance. We wandered through the streets long enough for me to buy a souvenir before departing.

We returned to Sanda's parents' home in Koper at about 8:30 that evening. Before entering the house, Sanda took me to her favorite place, their cherry orchard. We picked cherries from the tree and ate them. I felt like I was back in Michigan where I grew up. I used to pick fruit from the trees and eat it.

When we entered the house, Sanda's mom was busy in the kitchen preparing dinner. I told her there was not any room left in my stomach after the great lunch earlier and the cherries I had just eaten. She would not take "no" for an answer. A plate was placed in front of me and it was piled high with fish, rice, vegetables, and salad. I did my best to please her, eating most of the fish and salad. She has an incredible sense of humor and kept us all laughing during dinner.

Sanda's father came home late from a business meeting. He was a short man with a pleasant, bearded face. Although he was quiet, there was a warm friendliness about him.

I felt nostalgic being there in this family atmosphere. I missed my family. I knew I would be heading home in about six weeks and I knew I would be ready by then.

While at Sanda's, I called Elizabeth, our mutual friend in Vienna, Austria. She was pleased to hear from both of us. Knowing I was so close, she insisted that I come to stay with her for a few days. I agreed. She lived in the small town of Baden, about ten miles from Vienna, and worked in the city.

Sanda drove me to the capitol city of Ljubljana, located in the central part of the country. The next day we drove northwest to the Julian Alps. That day it rained sporadically. The on-again, off-again rain was pleasant. The clouds were lovely hanging over the Alps, and when the sun came out, the huge evergreens sparkled like diamonds.

We drove to the town of Bled. The Bled Castle perches atop a steep cliff 100 meters above the lovely lake. Another feature of Bled is a tiny island at the west end of the lake. We hired one of the hand-propelled gondolas to reach the island. They said that in the winter one can skate across the lake. In the rain, some of the beauty was lost but it was still very picturesque.

By the time I left Slovenia I had seen a large portion of the country, thanks to Sanda and Boris' kind hospitality. It is one of the loveliest countries I visited on that trip. Maybe I'll have the opportunity to return someday.

In the summer of 1996, I moved back to San Diego from Idaho. And I was blessed with a visit from Sanda. She stayed with me for a week, and had the opportunity to meet my family. She was especially taken with my granddaughters. By then I had two. I was pleased to have the opportunity to return her hospitality.

We stayed in touch for a number of years and then somehow we lost contact.

Austria

Sanda, on her way to work at the casino, drove me across the border to Gorizia, Italy, for the train to Vienna. The train ride was pleasant but long. The countryside was rather nondescript.

I called three hostels when I arrived in Vienna, and they were all full. Finally I found a budget hotel with a vacancy. Budget hotels were certainly more expensive in Europe than in Asia and India.

Once I was checked in and comfortably settled in my room I realized how calm I had been while I was calling all these places for a room. I had not panicked. I just kept calling another suggestion from my guide book. I had become a seasoned traveler. I had learned to just do the next indicated step to accomplish my goal. However, the problem with getting a room did indicate that maybe the summer season was beginning in Europe. I realized a phone call ahead was in order as I continued on my travels.

The next day I called Elizabeth; it was Saturday and she was home. She told me which train to take to Baden, about twenty-five minutes from Vienna. She would be at the station to meet me.

Elizabeth had lived all of her twenty-four years in Baden, Austria. It was a very pretty town with a population of about 30,000 in 1994. The town attracted the rich and retired, reminiscent of La Jolla, California, without the ocean.

On Saturday and Sunday afternoons, from spring to fall, there were concerts in the park in the middle of the town. It was filled with people sitting or strolling while they listened to the lovely music. The afternoon I was there they were playing songs from *My Fair Lady*.

Elizabeth's apartment was very spacious, with a couple of rooms that she did not use. The building belonged to her parents, so she was secure in her residence. She invited me to stay in her apartment instead of the hotel in Vienna. So I checked out of the hotel and moved into one of the rooms in her apartment.

Elizabeth invited a few of her friends over for tea and to sample a special Austrian cake she baked in my honor. They all spoke English. I had a wonderful evening and enjoyed meeting new friends in Vienna.

On Monday, Elizabeth went to work. The next few days I took the bus into Vienna to explore for the day and returned to Baden to have dinner with Elizabeth.

Since I was in Austria, with Czech Republic/Slovakia just across the border, a question came to mind. Should I visit my late husband's relatives who live in Slovakia? Before leaving on my trip I got the address for Aunt Emilia, a distant aunt of my husband's, from Florence, my sister-in-law. The aunt lived in Velky Saris and spoke no English. I also asked Florence to write a letter to Aunt

Emilia and tell her that I might come to visit the family while on my travels.

Knowing the family did not speak English, and I certainly did not speak Slovakian, would a visit be too uncomfortable for all of us? After mulling it over for a few hours, I decided I had come this far, why not stretch myself just a little farther and go see my late husband's extended family?

With Elizabeth's help we found the town of Presov on a map. From there it was about eight miles to Velky Saris. Checking the train schedules revealed one big drawback. I would have to change trains three times to reach Presov.

Mustering up my courage, I bought a ticket to Bratislava, the border town between the two countries. I boarded the first train at 6:00 the next morning. I changed trains in Bratislava. There I exchanged my Austrian shillings for Slovakian crowns so I could purchase my ticket on to Presov. When I purchased the ticket I was shocked. It cost only US$6.06! I was traveling halfway across that country for a little over $6.00 and the train ticket from Vienna had cost $43 for a one-hour ride!

After buying the ticket, I was confused as to which direction to go to find the platform for my train to Kysak, my next destination. I asked a few people and they did not speak English. I spotted a porter and asked him. I got a blank look. Obviously, he didn't speak English either.

Seeing my predicament, a lady approached and spoke to me in broken English. She was going in the same direction and asked me to follow her. Once on the train, she told another lady, in Slovakian, where I needed to get off, as she would be leaving the train before I would. As she got off at her stop I could tell, even though I could not understand her, that she was reminding the other lady to tell me when to get off.

The change in Kysak to the train to Presov could have been very confusing for me, but my "caretaker" put me in the hands of another lady who was going on to Presov. She guided me down the track to the correct train and we boarded.

In Presov she guided me to a taxi stand and explained to the driver that I wanted to go to Velky Saris. I showed him the address of the relatives and we were on our way.

When we arrived in the small town, the driver had not a clue as to where the street was located. We were at a disadvantage as we could not communicate with each other, either. About that time I saw two ladies waiting to cross the street. I motioned for him to stop and show them the address. When he did, their eyes lit up and they pointed down the street and to the right. He thanked them in his native language, smiled at me, and off we went.

Sure enough, two short blocks later we were in front of a house. There were three elderly women sitting in the yard. The driver got out of the car and took the photograph I had of my sister-in-law Florence with Aunt Emilia, and showed it to one of them. The lady grabbed the photo and started running toward the taxi with a big smile on her face. I knew I had found the relatives.

I got out of the taxi and she hugged me close. I could feel her tears on my cheek. I was so touched, tears welled up in my eyes as well.

I said, "Emilia?"

She replied, "Yes. Maria, Mike's wife?"

I could not talk but nodded my head in a positive response and we hugged again.

"Hotel?" I asked as I pointed to myself.

"No. Here." She responded.

I paid the driver and tried to thank him as best I could. I know he did not understand my language, but he did understand my gestures and the tip I gave him.

Those few words of English were about all Emilia knew. She dug out her Slovakian/English dictionary as we tried to communicate.

When her granddaughter, Martina, came by later that day, she was sent next door to get Peter, a high school student. Peter spoke English rather well. For the rest of the day and the next, he was our interpreter.

As we sat at the kitchen table Emilia shared with me, through Peter, that in this very house my father-in-law, Michael Steven Estocin, had lived. It was a powerful feeling to be sitting there amongst the roots of my late husband, as well as the roots of my three daughters and now my granddaughter.

I did not stay long, but the time I was there was special.

Once more I had been divinely guided. I was so grateful I had taken the chance to venture off the path. Meeting these wonderful, loving relatives was a huge treat that I would not have wanted to miss.

Peter and Emilia's son, Jan, took me into Presov to the train station. I booked a sleeper, with Peter's help, on an all-night train from Presov to Prague. The cost was about $18 to travel from the east to the west of the two countries. Trains were very inexpensive in Slovakia and the Czech Republic. Are trains still much cheaper there than in other parts of Europe? If I remember correctly I could not use my Eurail pass in this country.

I had a comfortable compartment and slept well. Getting off the train in Prague, I saw a sign that read "accommodations" but found they were closed. I took out my guide book just as a young man asked if I needed a room. He first quoted $25 a night but when I asked if there was a discount for three or four nights he said it would be $20 a night. That sounded just fine to me.

We boarded a trolley and in no time I was in the residence where I would be for the next few days. It was not a room, but a spacious one-bedroom apartment with twin beds in the bedroom, a small sitting room, and a lovely kitchen with the sun shining brightly in the window. I paid and thanked the young man and he left.

It was still morning and I had the whole day ahead of me. I turned on the stove to heat water for tea, then sat down to enjoy the luxury of being alone in my own apartment.

I loved Prague. It is a magical old city, filled with charm and history. Again, it's a city best seen on foot. I walked and walked and walked.

One of my highlights while in Prague was the St. Charles Bridge. And it was all I had expected it to be. The artists were all around with their creations for sale. The singers and musicians were sharing their talent and hoping for tips from the spectators.

I took a train to Karlovy Vary, also in the Czech Republic. It is known for its hot mineral pools. All I found when I arrived was a large outdoor swimming pool. Perhaps the hot mineral baths are for the ill who check into the resort.

I realized I knew where to go to find some hot mineral baths; it was time to go.

Germany

After my entry into Germany I spent five hours in Stuttgart roaming around and seeing the sights before boarding the train for Baden-Baden. Reading my guide book a while back, I had stumbled upon Baden-Baden and the Caracalla Pools. That is how I knew where I wanted to go. I was very tired after so many months of traveling and a few days of rest in the hot mineral baths of Baden-Baden were definitely the therapy I needed at the moment.

I called The Jugendherberge (the German word for youth hostel) from Stuttgart. They did not take phone reservations, but I was told there was a good chance a bed would be available.

From the train station in Baden-Baden I took the Number One bus to the general area of the youth hostel. I was in for a big surprise when I started walking to the hostel. It was all uphill! It was twenty minutes before 6:00 and the desk was closing at 6:00 and would not open again until 8:00 that evening.

Huffing, puffing, and dripping with perspiration, I arrived at the hostel a little after 6:00. The desk was closed so there was nothing to do but wait and hope a bed would be available.

Making the best of an uncomfortable situation, I found a ladies' room and washed the sweat from my face, neck, and arms, then went outside. Not wanting to leave the premises, I sat down to socialize with others also waiting to check in.

I had a banana and some cookies in my backpack, so I ate them for dinner. I had eaten a large lunch that day so a snack was sufficient.

As I waited with the other travelers, I looked around and found the surroundings to be rather serene. There were tall trees all around to help keep the buildings cool. Everything appeared to be neat and tidy.

I was able to check in at 8:00 that evening and found that my dorm room was on the fifth floor. Yep, no lift. I had to walk up five flights of stairs. By the time I reached my bunk, I was in desperate need of a shower. After scrubbing off the sweat and grime, I climbed between the crisp, clean sheets and fell asleep immediately.

I loved Baden-Baden. The baths more than met my expectations. The first day there I went to the Friedrichsbad, the old Roman-Irish bath house.

I was escorted into a changing room where I took off all my clothing and was then issued a locker in which to store my belongings. With the locker key tied to my wrist, and wearing nothing else, I walked to the baths. A lady met me with a towel and a pair of bath slippers. She gestured to a stall shower and told me to take a hot shower. In the shower area I read a sign of instructions. This would be a fifteen-level procedure.

No. 1 was the hot shower. No. 2, a hot sauna at 54 degrees centigrade, which is 129 degrees farenheit, then into another sauna at 154 degrees farenheit. No. 4 was me lying on a table while one of the attendants scrubbed my entire body with a brush, thick with soap. Then she gave me a short massage. No. 5 was a steam room, then into a very hot pool.

Following the hot pool I was led to a number of other pools, each one slightly cooler. The last one felt freezing cold to me. It was 64 degrees farenheit. I was grateful it was just a quick dip.

A friendly attendant wrapped me in a heated blanket and escorted me to a room filled with cots. I was instructed to lie down while she wrapped another warm blanket around me. The attendant told me to rest for a half-hour. I was there for forty-five minutes. I was so comfortable, I dozed off.

After almost three hours of being completely pampered, it was time to leave. I walked out of the Roman Baths with weak knees from being so relaxed. All this had only cost me US$20.

Stopping at a market, I bought bananas, apples, and a small loaf of dark German bread, then walked to the park. As I sat on a bench, enjoying my lunch and feeling so very relaxed, I found myself thinking about home. It was mid-June. I had been gone for nine months. I was getting tired of traveling and I missed my family.

After lunch I booked a flight from Zurich to London, leaving on July 6. This gave me about three more weeks to see whatever else I was going to see in Europe. I would spend a couple of days in London and likely see my friend Peter.

The next day I went to the Caracalla Pools and Spa, a coed, bathing-suit-required spa. Some of the pools were undercover but the larger ones were outdoors.

As I entered the warm, bubbling outdoor pool, I glanced up and looked into a pair of sparkling eyes. The owner of these eyes was an attractive man and he was smiling at me. I smiled back before moving over to another area of the pool. In a very short time he was sitting next to me. After a few moments I asked if he spoke English and he shook his head and replied, „No, Français."

Another man joined us. I noticed that his English was flawless when he introduced himself as Gerard. Quickly he introduced his friend.

"His name is Christian, and he does not speak English."

The two men were in Baden-Baden on business. They worked for a men's clothing factory in France and were in town to sell merchandise to local clothing stores.

I really enjoyed the pool and the company of Christian and Gerard. Although Christian and I didn't speak the same language, we swam together, and splashed each other and laughed a lot. When I entered the spa, I paid for two hours, and in what seemed like a few minutes my time was up.

I said good-bye to my new friends. We agreed that if their schedule allowed, they would meet me there the next day.

I showered and dressed. When I came out of the ladies' locker room, Gerard and Christian were waiting for me. They invited me to have a drink with them in a cafe nearby. I ordered a cafe au lait, and the two men ordered beer.

The conversation was light but somewhat strained. Gerard spoke for both himself and Christian. I could tell he was trying to be a matchmaker, but with the language barrier between Christian and me his efforts were not working.

Gerard insisted that Christian and I exchange addresses. I spoke no French so therefore could not correspond with him in French. I reasoned that if Christian wrote to me I could get someone at home to translate for me. We said good-bye with the thought that we could meet again the next day in the pools.

As I walked back to the hostel that evening I kept humming, "What a day this has been, What a rare mood I am in. It's almost like being in love."

I knew it was not love, but I had been very attracted to and comfortable with this handsome Frenchman with whom I could not communicate properly.

They were not at the pools the next day. That was my last day in Baden-Baden. I dropped Christian a card after I returned to the United States but he never replied. C'est la vie...

Switzerland

I arrived in Lucerne, Switzerland a little after 1:00 in the afternoon on June 21, the first day of summer.

I changed money and picked up a map of the town and a train schedule for my other Swiss destinations. I had called ahead for a hotel reservation at the Linde Hotel and found it to be very near the train station. A short walk led me to my small, but sparkling clean room on the third floor of this convenient hotel, in the heart of the old city. Lucerne was an enjoyable city enhanced with a river flowing through the town, which fed into a very large lake.

Being in Switzerland brought out the "buying fever" in me. I saw so many intriguing small gifts for my family. I looked at the prices and shuddered. Things were expensive in Switzerland! But I still purchased a number of gifts.

I took a day trip to explore the villages and sights on Lucerne Lake. I stayed on the ferry all the way to the end just to see the sights. On the return I got off at the village of Vitznau. Earlier I had seen a gondola that went all the way to the top of the mountain and I wanted to go there.

I had a hard time finding the gondola. When I finally found it, there was not a person in sight to ask about riding it to the top. I was a little hesitant to go up by myself. Then I noticed a sign in English giving a phone number to call for instructions on operating the gondola. A male voice answered. He told me exactly what to do, and that he would be at the top to meet me. Still feeling a little reluctant to go up alone, I once again brought my favorite slogan to mind, *Feel the Fear and Do It Anyway*!

In a couple of minutes I was in the gondola on my way up the steep mountain. It was a little hazy, but the view was awesome. At the top, the man was there to meet me as promised. He escorted me to a secluded and peaceful restaurant. On the floor in the dining room there was a baby fawn asleep next to a large, lovable dog. I was told this establishment was also a hostel, but I didn't get the name. I ordered a fresh green salad and tea. After eating lunch and sipping the tea while enjoying the view, I took the gondola back down.

On the return cruise, the boat stopped at other little villages to pick up or let off passengers. The return trip seemed to take forever.

Once back in the town, I discovered a rather inexpensive place for dinner. They had nachos on the menu! My favorite fatty food! I ordered nachos and a green salad. I forced myself to stay awake until 9:30 that night. It had been an enjoyable day, but all the fresh air and sun from 9:00 in the morning until 7:00 that evening had drained me.

I left Lucerne by train and was treated to a breathtaking ride to Interlaken. The two cities are a little over fifty miles apart, but because the train stopped so many times along the way it took two hours. I enjoyed every minute of the scenic ride. The beauty of the rugged white snow-capped mountains, and of lakes that are as blue as a robin's eggs, and little villages nestled in the green countryside, were a treat that I did not want to end.

But end it did as the train slowly made its way into Interlaken. I had a reservation at the local hostel. I was told that it was Switzerland's first private hostel and about a fifteen-minute walk from the train station. With my heavy backpack it seemed farther. Once there, I was more than satisfied. I was assigned a lower bunk in a girls' dorm, then went out to look around.

Interlaken is located on two lakes. The area is quite spread out because the lakes are separated by the town. In order to see everything I wanted to see, I rented a bike. I thoroughly enjoyed the outdoorsy atmosphere of Interlaken. I guess that's why they have such a large hostel, as the area attracted the young and the young at heart like me.

After exploring the two lake areas I signed up for a day-trip to Grindelwald for a hike to Faulhorn. I took a gondola up as far as I could and then started the hike. The path took me through mud and, many times, snow, but the air was not cold. I wore shorts and a short-sleeved t-shirt with a sweater over my shoulders and was comfortable.

I climbed for about two hours and still had not reached my destination when it started to rain. Too much mud and slippery snow ended the hike. I walked back to the gondola, rode part way, then got off and walked the rest of the way down. It was raining but not hard enough for me to pull out my umbrella.

Being in Interlaken reminded me how much I love being out in nature and hiking. I had not been sure where I was going next but now I knew—Zermatt, the home of the Matterhorn.

Beautiful, with a great big capital "B", is not adequate to describe Zermatt, Switzerland. From the time I boarded the special Red Train at the station in Brig, I was overwhelmed with the extraordinary scenery.

Once in Zermatt, I chose a hotel directly across the street from the train station. I asked for a single but all they had was a four-bed dorm. As it turned out, I was the only occupant of the room.

While exploring the area I was treated to my first view of the Matterhorn. I took numerous photographs of the famous mountain from various angles. I snapped shots during the clear early morning, the late afternoon, while the mountain was encircled with clouds, and in the evening shadows. What a glorious subject the Matterhorn is for photographers!

The next day, as I purchased a ticket for the tram, I asked if I could rent skis up top, in case I chose to go skiing.

The ticket seller smiled and said, "Ya."

One tram and two gondolas later, I was at the top.

I was disappointed when I was told there were no ski rentals. Skis must be rented in the village before coming up. The fare had been $40 so I knew this was my one and only trip up in the tram. By now I had learned to deal with my disappointments as well as my successes. I chose to enjoy the opportunity to take more photographs.

I saw a sign near an elevator that read, "Lift to observation point." I took the lift up and walked out into winter wonderland. Down below there had not been any snow, but up here it was all white. I saw the skiers in the distance and felt a pang of jealousy, but in the next moment I let it go and relaxed and enjoyed the remarkable view. A feeling of gratitude for just being there flooded over me.

As I was riding the gondola down from the top I got off at the first stop to have lunch. I sat outdoors on the verandah enjoying the warm sun and the magnificent view of the Matterhorn. I felt warm and toasty, unlike on top where it was quite cold and windy.

After lunch I found a hiking trail near the restaurant. I hiked for a couple of hours before the altitude began to have an effect. I was very tired as I boarded the second gondola down to catch the tram for the final descent into the village.

The next day I rented a bike. Bike riding on the Zermatt terrain was not easy. I found I was not as fit as I thought. After about three hours I returned the bike and did the rest of my exploring by foot. It would be wonderful if they have electric bikes there nowadays.

Cars are not allowed in Zermatt. The only mode of transportation is a small electric car. Those were their taxis. I found everything I needed to be in walking distance so I did not hire one.

Hiking around Zermatt is superb. I hiked through a place called the Gorge, a two-and-one-half-hour walk. There was a nominal fee to enter. The water rushing through the gulch makes it not only beautiful, but also exciting. The hike ended at a restaurant. I sat down to eat and savor the feelings and thoughts of the adventure I just experienced.

Zermatt is made for the lover of the outdoors and nature. I wasn't able to ski the Matterhorn that trip, but all the other superb attractions made up for that one small disappointment. And to this day I still haven't skiied there and probably never will.

After Zermatt it was time to continue north towards Zurich. I called Denise, the Servas host in Zurich, to see if I could stay with her once again. She said she would be delighted.

I stopped off in Bern for a short time. I checked my large backpack at the train station. Switzerland was having a heat wave and I did not need to carry the extra weight. The youth hostel was quite a walk from the train station and even without my large pack I was drenched with sweat by the time I reached it. The hostel was clean and well organized, in fact, probably one of the nicest of the entire trip. The YMCA in Hong Kong was a close second.

I walked down by the river and watched people enjoying themselves in the water. The river had a strong, swift current which towed them downstream for a bit, then they would get out and walk back to start again. It looked so refreshing and such fun, but where was my bathing suit? At the train station in my backpack. Oh, well, just being a spectator was fun enough.

Bern was not my favorite Swiss city. The guide book mentioned "druggies" in Bern. As I walked through the parks, that was quite obvious. The addicts had their straws and needles out in plain sight as they used them. That short time in Bern was plenty for me.

I arrived in Zurich near noon the next day. Denise, my Servas host, would not be home from work until after 6:00 that evening. I took this opportunity to take care of some travel business.

I went to the Swiss Airlines office to confirm my reservation to London. From London I would be transferring to Delta Airlines and would re-enter the United States, in Miami, Florida. Yes, I would be returning soon to the United States.

I called London and made a reservation at the Victoria Hotel near the Victoria train station.

I called my friend, Hazel, and found she would be in Greece with her boyfriend when I arrived. I was disappointed. She and I had become such good friend in Malaysia and during the time we spent together in Bali and Ubud before she had to return home. I would miss seeing her while in England. But since then I have been blessed to rendezvous with her in London and also Paris. We are still in touch.

I called Peter, the man I had met in Thailand. Peter was happy to hear from me and asked me to call when I arrived in London. He would catch a train in from Essex to show me around London town.

Once I knew I would be in Miami, I called my childhood friend, Frieda, who lived in nearby Hollywood, Florida. I would spend a few days with her and also my nephew, who lives near Miami on Marathon Key. I gave Frieda my flight number and told her I would be arriving in Miami on July 8. I asked her to call my nephew, Fred, with my arrival information.

By the time I finished my travel arrangements, had lunch, and made all those phone calls, it was almost time to take the tram to Denise's flat. It was still hot, so Denise made a refreshingly cool lettuce salad for dinner. We had a pleasant evening catching up on all the happenings of the past few months.

That night it rained, which helped cool off the streets temporarily. The next morning the sun was shining brightly and the heat returned. When Denise came home from work, we put on our bathing suits and went to Lake Zurich for a swim. I found this fascinating, as the last two times I had been to Zurich it had been quite cold, and now there I was swimming in the lake!

After the swim, I treated Denise to dinner. We went to her favorite restaurant atop a hill. I do not remember the name but what remains in my mind is the lovely view of Zurich below and Denise's pleasant company.

The next day, before taking the train to the airport, I went shopping for Swiss chocolates. When I called my daughter, Suzie, from the airport, she was so excited about the chocolates that I bought four more boxes. I could not leave Switzerland without an ample supply of chocolates for my loved ones and for myself.

London

When I arrived in London, I was content in the fact that I was on my way home, but first, my friend Peter was going to show London to me. What a treat, seeing London with an Englishman!

The weather was a welcome change from Switzerland. It was 70 degrees F. I arrived in London in mid-afternoon and found my hotel without a problem. I called Peter. We made plans to spend the next day together. He would "fetch me" at my hotel at 10:00 the next morning and we would see London town.

Peter arrived promptly. He had grown a mustache since I had last seen him. It was very attractive.

We walked to Victoria Station and purchased an all-day pass good for the underground or buses. With our inexpensive pass in hand we were ready to go.

Peter showed me so much of London. We walked by Big Ben and the Parliament Building. We walked on Tower Bridge and past the Tower of London, a prison years ago.

We took a bus past Trafalgar Square. We went to St. Paul's Church and climbed to the top of the Cathedral. We ate lunch at Wren Christopher's Pub, the man who designed St. Paul's. We visited Piccadilly Circus. We sat in a park across from Buckingham Palace to listen to music and eat ice cream cones. We went to the Hyde Park area so I could visit the Hard Rock Cafe's gift shop to buy my daughter, Suzie, another Hard Rock Cafe t-shirt.

We returned to Victoria Station a little after 9:00 that evening. I checked the train schedule for the next morning's trip to the airport. Peter suggested we have dinner at Garfunkel's, a restaurant across the street from Victoria Station.

It had been a fun day. Peter said he had loved showing me his town as well as seeing it again himself. And I had enjoyed the company of this nice, easy-to-be-with English gentleman.

The day had been an enjoyable send-off for me. Now, after ten months of traveling, I was returning to the United States to the warmth and love of my family and friends.

Peter and I exchanged addresses and wrote for a number of months. Then he wrote me a letter telling me he was engaged, and our communication ended.

The United States!

The first person I saw when I returned to United States soil in Miami was my dearest friend, Frieda. We have known each other since the fourth grade. She met me at Miami International Airport, then we drove to Marathon Key to visit my nephew, Fred.

Frieda and I spent two days with Fred in his home right on the water in Marathon Key. After our visit with him we drove to Frieda's home in Hollywood, Florida. After five days enjoying my dear friend Frieda's company, it was time to leave.

We said good-bye knowing we would see each other the next summer in Michigan. We were meeting there to attend our fortieth class reunion of Benton Harbor High School.

Next stop, California!

I was excited as I boarded Delta Airlines Flight 877 bound for Los Angeles. The long-awaited day had arrived. I was going home!

Suzie was there to meet me. I cried when I saw her, the youngest of my three daughters, my baby.

My middle daughter, Jane, was on location in Colorado. I was saddened that I would not be seeing her for a few more months. When we drove up in front of my oldest daughter's home, I saw Kathy, her husband Steve, and my little grandchild Clara, looking out the widow and waving at me. I read Steve's lips, "Clara, there is your Grandma!" Now my granddaughter is called Storm, one of her middle names.

I rushed up the stairs, opened the door, and entered. I saw my small granddaughter running toward me with a big smile on her face and her arms open wide. I knelt down and in a moment felt her warm, soft body in my arms and a sweet, moist kiss on my cheek.

She didn't stay in my arms long, but those few moments were enough. Yes, I was home—home with my family! My heart felt so full, I thought it might burst at any moment.

I was in awe of my granddaughter. I had left behind a little baby of seven months, only to return to find a toddler of seventeen months, walking and talking.

When I talked to my daughter, Jane, who handled my finances while I was away, I found I had money in my account. Not only had I stayed within my budget while traveling, I had actually saved money. I had a few thousand dollars in the bank. It had cost less money to live each month on the road than I normally spent each month at home. I kept an accounting of most of my expenditures and calculated the entire trip to have cost me a little over $20,000. I would have spent more than that in a ten-month period if I had been home. I was elated!

After the excitement of being with my family subsided I warily approached the scale. Now my mood went from exhilaration to depression. I had gained almost ten pounds! All those delicious breads and excellent pastries I enjoyed in Europe had come back to haunt me. Even though I did a lot of exercise it wasn't enough to make up for the extra calories. Fortunately, I knew all I had to do was watch what I ate for a few weeks and exercise each day and the extra pounds would disappear.

Being around Clara (Storm) certainly helped me with the exercise part. She was a very active, outgoing little girl and keeping up with her was tiring. I took her to swimming class and my heart filled with pride. She, of course, was the best one in the class. I took her to the park. She had no fear of the slides, going up and down, laughing all the while.

After a few weeks with my family in California, I drove to my home in Idaho, but a large part of my heart remained in California with my daughters and my grandchild.

My middle daughter, Jane, had moved to Idaho a few years before. So before going to Sandpoint I stopped in Moscow, Idaho to visit her and her fiancé. I spent a few days with them and I took the opportunity to thank her for taking care of my finances.

My next stop was home and the end of my around-the-world adventure.

Epilogue

I am grateful for my health that allowed me the opportunity to travel the world. The people and the experiences I encountered in those ten months will remain with me for the rest of my life.

Mine was a divinely guided trip. God did for me, many times, the things I could not have done for myself. Anytime I felt lost or afraid, someone or something came to my rescue. I was never alone on that trip even though sometimes I felt as though I was.

After traveling successfully for ten months out of the country, alone, I knew I could do the same within my own country. After seeing the world, I wanted to see more of the United States. The following May, 1995, I rented out my home and took a four-month car trip to explore the United States.

In an effort to keep my expenses low, I stayed with family and friends along the way. When I did not know anyone, I called a Servas host. Again, I was treated like a long-lost friend by the Servas members. At times I chose a budget hotel or stayed in a hostel.

I ended that trip in California, arriving only a few weeks before the birth of my second granddaughter, Rowan Marie! She arrived on October 18, 1995. Now the joys of being a grandma were doubled. With two granddaughters to enjoy, I decided to move back to San Diego to be closer to my two daughters who live in California and the little ones. My daughter, Jane, is still living in Idaho with her husband, Pete. We stay in touch with phone calls, emails, and visits to one another.

So to each and every one of you who is reading this book, if you have the desire to travel, I encourage you to go. Either go alone, or find a companion. Just *"Feel the Fear and Do it Anyway!"*

About the Author

Quay Marie Estocin grew up in a small town in Michigan. She did not travel in her youth. But somewhere deep inside a child's heart was a spirit that longed to see the world. At eighteen she packed her bags and moved to San Diego, California. A year later she met a naval aviator. They were married and had three daughters. This marriage was cut short. Her husband was shot down over North Vietnam and became a hero of that conflict. After the loss of her husband and the launching of her daughters she began a life that has taken her around the world both physically and spiritually several times. From Australia to Canada, from Africa to Japan. Marie Estocin has experienced the distant corners of the earth where she met people from all walks of life. Her travels encouraged her to write this book. Marie is an active woman, she plays tennis, golf and use to ski. Marie's life has simply been a journey of courage and adventure whose destiny was to understand what it means to be human. She continues to travel today.

www.ingramcontent.com/pod-product-compliance
Lightning Source LLC
Chambersburg PA
CBHW021503090426
42739CB00007B/442